LET US PRAY

BIDDING PRAYERS FOR YOUNG PEOPLE

KATIE THOMPSON

First published in 2001 by
KEVIN MAYHEW LTD
Buxhall
Stowmarket
Suffolk IP14 3BW

0 1 2 3 4 5 6 7 8 9

ISBN 1 84003 683 4
Catalogue No 1500407

Cover design by Jonathan Stroulger
Edited by Katherine Laidler
Typesetting by Louise Selfe
Printed and bound in Great Britain

CONTENTS

PART TWO: The teaching of Jesus

PART THREE: Following Jesus

INTRODUCTION

'In truth I tell you, if two of you on earth agree about anything to ask,
it will be granted to you by my Father in heaven.
For where two or three gather in my name,
I am there with them.'
Matthew 18:19-20

These memorable words of Jesus are particularly relevant on any occasion when a group of individuals come together to pray. Intercessory prayer, in particular, helps us to remember that God is the source of all we have and everything we are. We do not pray to remind God of what we need; instead we need to pray to remind ourselves that he alone provides for all our needs, however large or small those needs might be.

As we remember God's loving goodness, we have the confidence to ask him for even more expressions of that love in our lives and world. Such prayers are a mix of 'large' and 'small' petitions, which range from worldwide concerns to matters of more personal interest. God is Lord of all these things. We ask for the 'big' things for all of humanity, before asking for the more specific needs of our own families and communities.

The petitions themselves are not mini-prayers addressed to God, but biddings or invitations by which we are asked to pray for certain people and situations. We try to pray as best we can for the needs of the whole world, and to trust in God's will and incredible love to do what is right for us. In this way we unite our love to God's own love for others, and because of our own concern for one another, we allow God to use us to make a difference in the world.

Each set of prayers begins with a brief invitation to pray, followed by a series of intentions or petitions for which everyone is invited to pray. Young people share in the prayer at their own level, and are encouraged to meditate briefly as they raise their thoughts for a moment to God. Short intervals of silence, combined with a suitable atmosphere for prayer, help to foster reflection and to develop personal encounters with God. Sometimes a relevant picture or image can prove to be a helpful focus. In appropriate circumstances a group can be invited and encouraged to offer their own individual and spontaneous petitions to be prayed for by everyone.

Praying with Christ and through Christ, the Holy Spirit is present within us as we offer our intercessions for ourselves and others. By becoming more sensitive to those in need, we are motivated and moved by him to do something to help. After all, prayer in action is love, and love in action is service.

The intercessions conclude with a prayer which is addressed to God (the Father) and made through Christ (the Son), as a general expression of our trust in God's goodness and love for us all.

This collection of prayers can be used as presented, or adapted to suit the needs of a particular group or gathering. Occasionally it may be necessary to shorten or rephrase some petitions to suit the attention span or individual experiences of younger children. I hope they will provide a useful starting point for sparking off thoughts and ideas for adding your own prayers.

The intercessions are arranged in themed sections which can be used at morning assemblies, services of prayer or other gatherings or celebrations with young people. Since prayers of intercession are a regular part of the Sunday liturgy of the Word, the Sunday Gospels have been linked thematically with a selection of appropriate prayers for you to choose from.

We all know that it is surprisingly difficult to try to think about what we are hearing or reading as we listen to or say the words of a prayer. Young people need to be nurtured and guided as we help them to understand that there is a difference between simply *saying* prayers and *praying* prayers.

Our part in prayer is to try to raise our hearts and minds to God. I hope these prayers of intercession offer a good place to start, helping to lift the spirits and enlighten the minds of young people as they learn to make room in their hearts and lives for the needs of others.

Katie Thompson

PART ONE

The Christian Life

1
FAITH

Faith is a mystery. Somehow it takes us where reason and common sense cannot go, and helps us to discover what lies beyond our simple human understanding. Faith is a gift from God which opens our hearts and minds to help us accept and believe the truth revealed by Christ. For this faith to live and grow in our everyday lives, we need the help of God's grace and the gifts of the Holy Spirit. Sometimes our faith can be uncertain and let us down at difficult times of our lives, but God understands and forgives any moments of weakness.

Have faith

As God's children,
we turn to our heavenly Father who loves us,
with all our troubles and needs:

For the Church and all her ministers;
that their faith in God's universal love
will help them in their mission
to share his Word with the world.

Silence

Lord, we believe:
Strengthen our faith.

For peace in our world and our lives;
that our faith in God's gift of peace
will allow us to bring pardon where there is injury
and forgiveness where there is hatred.

Silence

Lord, we believe:
Strengthen our faith.

For people who are filled with doubt and uncertainty;
that the faithful witness of Mary and Joseph her husband
will help them to walk from the darkness of doubt
into the light of certainty.

Silence

Lord, we believe:
Strengthen our faith.

For those who need to be forgiven or show forgiveness;
that our faith in God's desire and power
to forgive our sins and make us forgiving people
will change our hearts and lives for ever.

Silence

Lord, we believe:
Strengthen our faith.

For those who have died and departed from this world;
that their faith in Christ,
who is the Resurrection and the Life,
will lead them to everlasting life in the kingdom of heaven.
Especially we pray for .....

Silence

Lord, we believe:
Strengthen our faith.

Knowing that our heavenly Father is listening,
in the silence of our hearts
let us share our own unspoken prayers with him.

Silence

Heavenly Father,
faith helps us to pray,
and prayer helps us to believe.
Enliven our faith,
and warm our hearts with the love
which leads to eternal life with you.
We ask this through Christ your Son.
Amen.

Merciful Father, accept these prayers for the sake of your son, our saviour, Jesus Christ.

For those who are sick in mind, body or spirit & those who care for them. Especially we pray for ....
Bring them your peace in their pain, your strength in their weakness, & your comfort in their sadness.
LORD WE BELEIVE.
STRENGTHEN OUR FAITH.

With faith, nothing is impossible

Gathered together as the family of God,
let us bring the burdens and worries
which we carry through life
before the Father who loves and cares for us:

We pray for an end to hatred, prejudice
and fear in our world;
let us work together as brothers and sisters
to build God's kingdom of peace.

Silence

Lord of love:
We believe in you.

We pray for an end to oppression
and exploitation of the poor and the vulnerable;
let us work together to ensure a fairer world
which cares for the weak and the homeless.

Silence

Lord of love:
We believe in you.

We pray for all who hold and teach the Christian faith;
let us be filled with the Holy Spirit
and proclaim by our daily lives
the love which is firmly rooted and growing in our hearts.

Silence

Lord of love:
We believe in you.

We pray for the sick and all who struggle with pain;
let their faith in our heavenly Father's almighty power
bring them healing and comfort.

Silence

Lord of love:
We believe in you.

Knowing that our heavenly Father is listening,
in the silence of our hearts
let us share our own unspoken prayers with him.

Silence

Almighty God,
you change the lives of all who believe in you
and trust in your loving power.
Increase our faith
and make our lives a perfect offering to you.
We make these and all our prayers
through Christ your only Son, our Lord.
Amen.

Make our faith grow

Let us ask God to listen to the prayers of his people
gathered here together in love:

That ordained and lay people
who live and teach the Christian faith
may touch the hearts of others
and help them to understand God's Word
and to nurture their gift of faith.

Silence

Heavenly Father:
Help our faith to grow.

That people whose lives and livelihoods
have been ruined by disaster or conflict
may have their battered faith restored and refreshed,
as we respond to their needs
with practical aid to relieve their suffering.

Silence

Heavenly Father:
Help our faith to grow.

That countries which are struggling to rebuild communities
divided by war and hatred
may never lose faith or hope
in efforts to achieve peace and reconciliation.

Silence

Heavenly Father:
Help our faith to grow.

That the people of God
who open their hearts and minds to his Word
may allow him to lead us towards deeper faith,
greater hope and more generous love.

Silence

Heavenly Father:
Help our faith to grow.

Knowing that our heavenly Father is listening,
in the silence of our hearts
let us share our own unspoken prayers with him.

Silence

God our Father,
we ask you to hear our prayers.
Bless us with your love and compassion.
Send your Holy Spirit
to set our hearts alight
with the flames of faith and love.
We ask this in the name of Christ our Lord.
Amen.

2
LOVE

Jesus said, 'Love one another as I have loved you' (John 15:12). By his words and actions, he gave us the perfect example of how to love God and each other. Loving someone is not always easy; it demands that we are selfless, generous and forgiving. Love wants to give as much as it receives. Jesus calls us to look for and discover what is good and lovable hidden in every person we meet, however difficult that might sometimes be.

Love changes everything

Jesus taught us to call God 'Our Father'
and to ask him for all our needs.
So, with confidence in his love, we pray for one another:

Let the world in which we live be transformed by love;
may peace overcome war,
friendship replace loneliness
and selfishness turn to generosity.

Silence

God our Father:
Change our lives with your love.

Let the lives of the poor and those in need
be transformed by love;
may each of us do whatever we can
to relieve their suffering and hardship,
and may we never take for granted
what we are fortunate to have.

Silence

God our Father:
Change our lives with your love.

Let the Church and her people be transformed by love;
may we shine in the darkness of our world
and brighten the lives of others,
filling them with joy and hope.

Silence

God our Father:
Change our lives with your love.

Let suffering and pain be transformed by love;
may God's healing love bring comfort and strength
in times of loneliness and despair.

Silence

God our Father:
Change our lives with your love.

Knowing that our heavenly Father is listening,
in the silence of our hearts
let us share our own unspoken prayers with him.

Silence

Heavenly Father,
you generously pour out your love into our lives.
By willingly sharing that love
with our brothers and sisters everywhere,
may our lives be pleasing to you.
Grant this through Christ our Lord.
Amen.

In need of love

Knowing that God listens to the needs of his children
and answers our prayers,
together we pray:

That Christians everywhere
will live the forgiving love of Jesus
who welcomed sinners, befriended the tax collectors,
and cast stones at no one.

Silence

Lord, we pray:
For those who need your love.

That our family the Church
will share the love of Jesus
by helping those who have lost their way
to rediscover God's endless love.

Silence

Lord, we pray:
For those who need your love.

That broken homes and families
will find the love of Jesus
which heals wounds and brings fresh hope
where there is anger and despair.

Silence

Lord, we pray:
For those who need your love.

That, as caretakers of creation,
we will look for and see the love of God
reflected in the world around us,
and take responsibility for protecting and cherishing
all living creatures.

Silence

Lord, we pray:
For those who need your love.

Knowing that our heavenly Father is listening,
in the silence of our hearts
let us share our own unspoken prayers with him.

Silence

Lord God,
help us to recognise you
in the world around us,
and, by our living love,
to show how much we care for you.
Grant this through Christ your Son.
Amen.

3
SERVICE

Jesus constantly showed us how to serve God and one another by his loving example. We have been created to love others just as he loves us. 'Whatever you do to the least of my brothers, you do it to me' (Matthew 25:40). He gives us the opportunity to do for others what we would like to do for him – to put our love into living action. He makes himself the hungry one, the naked one, the homeless one, the sick one, the lonely one, the unwanted and rejected one.

Loving service

We come before our heavenly Father in love
to ask him to listen to the prayers of his children:

We pray that as Christians
we will serve God and one another
by becoming instruments of love in God's hands,
by feeding the hungry, clothing the naked
and befriending the homeless and unwanted.

Silence

Lord of love:
Help us to serve you.

We pray that we will be encouraged and inspired
by the lives of the Saints
and all who dedicate their lives to sharing
and living the Gospel of love.

Silence

Lord of love:
Help us to serve you.

We pray that we will satisfy our neighbour's hunger for love
by giving them a smile, sharing a glass of water,
or simply making time to talk and listen.

Silence

Lord of love:
Help us to serve you.

We pray that God will give us the strength and courage
to allow ourselves to go wherever he sends us,
and to do whatever he asks.

Silence

Lord of love:
Help us to serve you.

We pray that our eyes will open to see Christ
in the faces of our neighbours,
and that our hearts will open
to respond lovingly to their needs.

Silence

Lord of love:
Help us to serve you.

Knowing that our heavenly Father is listening,
in the silence of our hearts
let us share our own unspoken prayers with him.

Silence

Lord God,
you sent your beloved Son
to be our Servant King,
and to teach us your loving ways.
Fill us with the Holy Spirit
and help us to serve you and one another
according to your commandments of love.
We make our prayers through Christ our Lord.
Amen.

Love others as I love you

Gathered together as one loving family,
we ask our heavenly Father
to listen to the needs of all his children:

Let us pray for nations and people
who hunger for justice, equality and an end to poverty;
may we as Christians
recognise the dignity and rights of our neighbours
and do everything we can to satisfy and meet their needs.

Silence

Heavenly Father:
Increase our love.

Let us pray for people who thirst for peace and reconciliation;
may we commit ourselves
to work for international justice and peace
by defending human rights throughout the world.

Silence

Heavenly Father:
Increase our love.

Let us pray for people
who have been stripped of their dignity as human beings
by unemployment or homelessness;
may we clothe them with our compassion
and restore their hope and pride
by our efforts to relieve their suffering.

Silence

Heavenly Father:
Increase our love.

Let us pray for people who are imprisoned
by loneliness and fear;
may our friendship and love free them
to take their rightful place in the kingdom of God.

Silence

Heavenly Father:
Increase our love.

Let us pray for the sick and all who suffer;
may our visits and prayers comfort them,
and our loving care fill them with joy and hope.

Silence

Heavenly Father:
Increase our love.

Knowing that our heavenly Father is listening,
in the silence of our hearts
let us share our own unspoken prayers with him.

Silence

God our Father,
may we find the treasure of your loving kingdom
in the people and world around us.
We ask this in the name of Christ
who is Lord for ever and ever.
Amen.

4
HAPPINESS

God our Father wants us to be happy, and lasting happiness can be found when our hearts are filled with love and goodness. We all long to be happy with God in heaven at the end of our lives, but we can also be happy with him at this very moment. This means getting to know God better and loving as he loves, caring as he cares, giving as he gives, serving as he serves, and reaching out to touch the lives of others with the joy he pours into our lives.

Living happiness

Jesus taught us to call God 'Our Father'
and to ask him for all our needs.
So, with confidence in his love,
we pray for ourselves and others:

Blessed are those who hunger for what is just and fair;
may political leaders, citizens of rich countries
and Christians everywhere
ensure that we share the goods and resources of the world fairly,
for the happiness of all.

Silence

Merciful Lord:
Hear our prayer.

Blessed are those who work to bring peace to our world;
may they bring love where there is hatred,
forgiveness where there is anger,
and lasting happiness where there is sadness and despair.

Silence

Merciful Lord:
Hear our prayer.

Blessed are those who suffer
and are imprisoned for sharing the Good News;
may their faithful witness
fill them with happiness and consolation,
knowing that the kingdom of heaven belongs to them.

Silence

Merciful Lord:
Hear our prayer.

Blessed are the poor and homeless;
may they open our eyes, which are so often blinded
by selfishness and greed,
to see their needs and allow us to experience
the happiness which giving with love can bring.

Silence

Merciful Lord:
Hear our prayer.

Blessed are those who are saddened
by the loss of someone they love;
may their hope in the resurrection
and the promise of eternal life
bring them comfort, and turn their sadness to joy.

Silence

Merciful Lord:
Hear our prayer.

Knowing that our heavenly Father is listening,
in the silence of our hearts
let us share our own unspoken prayers with him.

Silence

Almighty God,
through Jesus your Son
you shared the secret of lasting happiness with us,
and showed us how to find and keep it.
By our words and actions in life,
may we enjoy eternal happiness in heaven.
We make our prayers through Christ our Lord.
Amen.

Be happy

Filled with love for God and one another,
let us pray together:

We pray for Christians throughout the world;
as faithful followers of Christ
may we find true happiness through serving God
and our brothers and sisters.

Silence

Father in heaven:
Grant our prayer.

We pray for the homeless, the hungry and the unemployed;
with our loving help and encouragement
may they find happiness in their troubled and difficult lives.

Silence

Father in heaven:
Grant our prayer.

We pray for an end to injustice, violence
and fear in our world;
may governments and leaders work tirelessly
for peace and equality
so that all people can enjoy the happiness they deserve.

Silence

Father in heaven:
Grant our prayer.

We pray for those who have died in the peace of Christ;
that they will enjoy the happiness of eternal life
with God in his heavenly kingdom.

Silence

Father in heaven:
Grant our prayer.

We pray for the families gathered here today;
let our homes and lives be filled with happiness and laughter
as we share the gift of God's love with one another.

Silence

Father in heaven:
Grant our prayer.

Knowing that our heavenly Father is listening,
in the silence of our hearts
let us share our own unspoken prayers with him.

Silence

Loving Father,
listen to our prayers
and answer them as you know best.
May the joy of Christ's resurrection
and your unending love
shine out from us as happiness
and touch the lives of others.
We ask this in the name of Christ our Lord.
Amen.

5
PEACE

Jesus said to his disciples, 'Peace is my gift to you, my own peace I give to you, a peace that the world cannot give' (John 14:27). Jesus is our peace. He overcomes division and hatred with love and forgiveness. As Christians we are called to love others as Christ loves us and to share his gift of peace with the world.

Peace be with you

Jesus told us to come to him like little children
with all our worries and troubles.
Let us pray now for our own needs
and the needs of our world:

We pray for the Church and all its people;
may we share the Gospel of peace by our living example
of acceptance, understanding and forgiveness.

Silence

Lord God:
Grant us your peace.

We pray for peacemakers in our world;
may we support their brave efforts
to heal injustice and reconcile differences and bitterness
in countries and communities divided by fear and hatred.

Silence

Lord God:
Grant us your peace.

We pray for those who are filled with doubt and uncertainty;
may they find faith in Jesus the risen Lord,
and be filled with the gift of his peace.

Silence

Lord God:
Grant us your peace.

We pray for families and homes
broken and damaged by violence and anger;
may they discover the healing peace of Christ
through our loving help,
and find the strength and courage to rebuild their lives.

Silence

Lord God:
Grant us your peace.

Knowing that our heavenly Father is listening,
in the silence of our hearts
let us share our own unspoken prayers with him.

Silence

God our Father,
you sent your beloved Son Jesus,
who is the Prince of Peace,
to transform our world with his love.
May our living love touch the lives of others
and bring them the gift of your peace.
We make our prayers through Christ our Lord.
Amen.

6
JOY

'Listen, I bring you news of great joy, a joy to be shared by all people' (Luke 2:10). This was the angel's greeting to the shepherds on the hillside as they announced the birth of a Saviour for the world. Jesus filled the lives of many with joy: he healed the sick, raised the dead to life, forgave sinners and befriended the friendless. We celebrate the joy of his glorious resurrection every Sunday as we recall his victory over death, and rejoice at his promise of eternal life.

Joy to the world

With simple trust and humble hope
we come before God our loving Father
with all our needs:

We pray for the leaders of the Church,
our government and the nations of the world;
that their wisdom and understanding
will fill people with hope for a better future in a fairer world.

Silence

Lord, in your love:
Fill us with joy.

We pray for those who have wandered away
from the love of families, friends and God;
that a change of heart will lead them to search
for those they have lost,
and rediscover the joy of love and reconciliation.

Silence

Lord, in your love:
Fill us with joy.

We pray for families whose children
have run away from home and are missing;
that they will succeed in their search to find them
and experience the joy of being reunited with those they love.

Silence

Lord, in your love:
Fill us with joy.

We pray for all Christian people;
that the peace and joy of Christ will grow in our hearts and lives
as we serve God and one another.

Silence

Lord, in your love:
Fill us with joy.

We pray for our loved ones who have died;
that they will be filled with the joy of the resurrection
as they share eternal glory with Jesus the Lord of life.

Silence

Lord, in your love:
Fill us with joy.

Knowing that our heavenly Father is listening,
in the silence of our hearts
let us share our own unspoken prayers with him.

Silence

Heavenly Father,
may we be filled with the joy of your love,
and gladly go out to share it with the whole world.
We ask this in the name of Christ our Lord.
Amen.

Fill us with joy

Gathered together in love,
as brothers and sisters in Christ,
let us ask our loving Father to listen to the prayers we make:

We pray for all newborn children and their families;
may God's wonderful gift of new life
fill their lives with love and joy.

Silence

God our Father:
Hear our prayer.

We pray for the world God has made;
may we care for and protect the gifts of creation
which bring us so much joy and pleasure.

Silence

God our Father:
Hear our prayer.

We pray for people who cure the sick and care for them;
may their skill and love bring comfort and happiness
to those who suffer.

Silence

God our Father:
Hear our prayer.

We pray for all who rest in peace with God;
may they be filled with unimaginable joy
as they live for ever with God in his heavenly kingdom.

Silence

God our Father:
Hear our prayer.

We pray for people who are alone and filled with despair;
may our friendship and love fill their lives
with joy and fresh hope.

Silence

God our Father:
Hear our prayer.

We pray for families and friends;
may our homes be places of forgiveness and friendship
where we share the joy and peace of God's love.

Silence

God our Father:
Hear our prayer.

Knowing that our heavenly Father is listening,
in the silence of our hearts
let us share our own unspoken prayers with him.

Silence

Loving Father,
fill our lives with joy
and help us to share all that you give us,
so that we can make this world
a happier place for everyone to live.
Grant this through Christ your Son.
Amen.

7
LIGHT

Without light in our world there would be little, if any, life. In some parts of the world, like Antarctica, the sun does not shine for six months of the year and there is complete darkness. Jesus is the 'Light of the world' (John 8:12) who came to chase away the darkness of sin, and light up the world with his life and love. At Baptism we become children of God, and are filled with the light of his living Spirit.

Light up our lives

As brothers and sisters in Christ,
we come together to ask our heavenly Father
to listen to the needs and concerns of all his children,
as we pray:

For all peoples and nations of the world;
may the light of Christ shining in our lives
help us to change the darkness of hunger, poverty and injustice
into the joy of sharing, caring and equality for everyone.

Silence

Lord of light:
Shine through us.

For the Church and her leaders;
may the light of Christ guide and direct them
to lead us to our loving Saviour,
just as the light from a star
directed the wise men on their journey.

Silence

Lord of light:
Shine through us.

For people who live in the darkness of hatred and fear;
may the light of Christ shining out from us
warm cold hearts and help others to see a new way forward
through forgiveness and friendship.

Silence

Lord of light:
Shine through us.

For our world and its many wonders;
may the light of Christ help us to glimpse the brightness

of God's glory reflected in the world around us,
and remind us to always treat his creation with care and respect.

Silence

Lord of light:
Shine through us.

For those who have died and those who miss them;
may the light of Christ and the promise of eternal life
turn the darkness of sadness
into the joy of hope and peace.

Silence

Lord of light:
Shine through us.

Knowing that our heavenly Father is listening,
in the silence of our hearts
let us share our own unspoken prayers with him.

Silence

Loving Father,
help us to always walk as children of the light,
shining out in the darkness,
and touching the lives of many
with the warmth of your love.
We make our prayers through Christ your Son.
Amen.

8
FAMILY

Love and sharing are at the heart of any family. Together we experience and share good times as well as bad times. Our families make us feel loved and safe, and our homes are usually where we first learn to forgive and be forgiven. When God became man, Jesus lived an ordinary family life in Nazareth with Mary and Joseph. They gave him the loving home and example which every child needs, but which not all are fortunate enough to enjoy. Through Baptism, we are welcomed as brothers and sisters into the one worldwide family of God.

Family life

As brothers and sisters in God's loving family,
let us ask God our heavenly Father
to listen to and answer the needs of all his children:

We pray for our family the Church
and all who are preparing for Baptism;
may we continue to grow in faith and love
as, filled with the Holy Spirit, we take our rightful place
in the one loving Body of Christ.

Silence

Loving Father:
Listen to the prayers of your family.

We pray for parents everywhere;
may their love for one another
be at the heart of family life,
protected from anything which might endanger it.

Silence

Loving Father:
Listen to the prayers of your family.

We pray for children throughout the world;
may they love and respect the parents who care for them,
and be blessed with happy homes
filled with forgiveness and understanding.

Silence

Loving Father:
Listen to the prayers of your family.

We pray for families
who are suffering the pain of separation and conflict;
may they find comfort and support

through the love and friendship
of their brothers and sisters in Christ.

Silence

Loving Father:
Listen to the prayers of your family.

Knowing that our heavenly Father is listening,
in the silence of our hearts
let us share our own unspoken prayers with him.

Silence

Loving Father,
in your tender love,
hear the prayers of your children.
Make us grow in love for you
and all our brothers and sisters.
We ask this through Christ our Lord.
Amen.

Broken families

Family life can sometimes be painful and difficult,
so let us pray to our heavenly Father
for the needs of families everywhere:

When families are forced to flee from danger or disaster,
may they draw strength
from the flight of the Holy Family into Egypt,
knowing that God will watch over them
and protect them from harm.

Silence

God of faith:
Heal our pain.

When families are pierced by a sword of pain and heartache,
may their suffering bring them closer in love to Mary,
who suffered as she watched her beloved Son dying on the cross.

Silence

God of compassion:
Heal our pain.

When families are divided,
may they never lose hope of being reunited in love,
just as Mary and Joseph were reunited with Jesus in the Temple
when all had seemed lost.

Silence

God of hope:
Heal our pain.

When families are weighed down by sickness and suffering,
may they be uplifted and filled with joy in their time of need,
by the loving support and help
of friends and family around them.

Silence

God of joy:
Heal our pain.

Knowing that our heavenly Father is listening,
in the silence of our hearts
let us share our own unspoken prayers with him.

Silence

Heavenly Father,
watch over and protect our families;
may the love we share
bring joy and hope to the world
and make it a better place.
We make our prayers through Christ our Saviour.
Amen.

Family blessings

Jesus taught us to call God 'Our Father'
and to ask him for all our needs.
Let us bring these needs before him now,
as we pray:

That God will bless the Christian family
gathered throughout the world to praise and worship him;
may we witness to his Gospel of love
by our words and actions.

Silence

Lord, hear us:
And bless our families.

That God will bless the leaders of every nation;
may they support families,
and hear and listen to their voices,
as they prepare to make political decisions.

Silence

Lord, hear us:
And bless our families.

That God will bless couples with the gift of children;
may they share their love for each other
within their own family,
and with the rest of the world.

Silence

Lord, hear us:
And bless our families.

That God will bless children everywhere
and keep them from danger and harm;
may parents, teachers and all who care for children
always do so with love and respect.

Silence

Lord, hear us:
And bless our families.

Knowing that our heavenly Father is listening,
in the silence of our hearts
let us share our own unspoken prayers with him.

Silence

Father of all,
accept our prayers
and help us to grow in faith and wisdom.
We ask this in the name of Christ your Son.
Amen.

9
MOTHERING SUNDAY

Being a mother is not always easy! Alongside the many joys which motherhood brings, mothers have their worries, their disappointments and a great deal of hard work. Often we take them and everything they do for us for granted. Today we pray for our Mother the Church, and for mothers everywhere who so faithfully dedicate their lives to loving and serving others, and to taking care of the families they love.

Motherly love

As brothers and sisters in God's loving kingdom,
we ask our heavenly Father
to listen to the needs of his children, as we pray:

For our Mother the Church;
may she be an example of forgiving love and deep faith
for all her children to follow.

Silence

Loving Father:
Hear our prayer.

For peace in our families and homes;
may we lovingly serve and respect one another,
and learn to forgive willingly and to be forgiven ourselves.

Silence

Loving Father:
Hear our prayer.

For mothers everywhere;
may we give thanks for their caring hands,
their loving hearts and for all the joy that they bring.

Silence

Loving Father:
Hear our prayer.

For those who mourn the loss of their mother;
may they find comfort in happy memories
and joy in the promise of eternal life and happiness.

Loving Father:
Hear our prayer.

Knowing that our heavenly Father is listening,
in the silence of our hearts
let us share our own unspoken prayers with him.

Silence

Almighty God,
may we live in Christ's love
by serving you and one another,
and never take the love we share for granted.
We make our prayers through Christ our Lord.
Amen.

PART TWO

The teaching of Jesus

10
THE KINGDOM OF GOD

The kingdom of God is very precious. Everyone can belong to this kingdom, wherever they live, however much or however little money they have, and whatever the colour of their skin. To live in this kingdom means that we must live as Jesus taught us, putting the love of God and our neighbour before everything else. As we grow in kindness, love, understanding and forgiveness, we share that kingdom with each other through our words and actions. In this way, day by day, we each play a part in helping the kingdom of God to grow.

Let the kingdom grow

As brothers and sisters in God's kingdom of love,
we ask our heavenly Father
to listen to the prayers of his children,
as we pray:

For all of God's family;
that the words of Jesus will take root in our hearts and lives
and make us grow in love for one another.

Silence

Father, hear our prayer:
Let your kingdom grow.

For the poor and the hungry;
that we who have plenty may always be ready
to help our brothers and sisters who have little.

Silence

Father, hear our prayer:
Let your kingdom grow.

For understanding, forgiveness and peace in our world;
that leaders and nations will work together
to build one kingdom of love.

Silence

Father, hear our prayer:
Let your kingdom grow.

For people who are sad or lonely;
that, like Jesus, we may always be ready to reach out to others
with a hand of friendship and a welcoming smile.

Silence

Father hear our prayer:
Let your kingdom grow.

Knowing that our heavenly Father is listening,
in the silence of our hearts
let us share our own unspoken prayers with him.

Silence

Heavenly Father,
fill us with your love,
so that your kingdom
will grow in us and through us.
We ask this through Jesus Christ our Lord.
Amen.

Let the kingdom come

Jesus taught us to pray to our heavenly Father,
'Thy kingdom come, thy will be done.'
With hope in the coming of God's kingdom,
let us turn to him with our needs and the needs of the world:

We pray for the Church throughout the world;
may God's kingdom come
in our daily lives as we live Christ's Gospel of love.

Silence

Lord, hear our prayer:
Let thy kingdom come.

We pray for people whose lives are shattered
by war or violence;
may God's kingdom come
through the efforts of all who work
to bring peace to troubled lives and nations.

Silence

Lord, hear our prayer:
Let thy kingdom come.

We pray for the sick and all who suffer;
may God's kingdom come
through the love and compassion
of all who visit and care for them.

Silence

Lord, hear our prayer:
Let thy kingdom come.

We pray for the homeless and the unemployed;
may God's kingdom come
through our love for one another,
as we help anyone who is in trouble or afraid.

Silence

Lord, hear our prayer:
Let thy kingdom come.

Knowing that our heavenly Father is listening,
in the silence of our hearts
let us share our own unspoken prayers with him.

Silence

Father,
make us grow in love for you and one another,
and give us the courage to do your will,
so that your kingdom may come.
Grant this through Christ your Son.
Amen.

Kingdom of love

When two or three gather together to pray,
God is there with them.
Knowing that he is listening,
let us bring the needs of ourselves and others before him,
as we pray:

For the Church and all God's people;
that having heard and understood
the Good News that Jesus came to share,
each of us in our own way
will share that message of hope and love
with the rest of the world.

Silence

Lord, in your love:
Listen to our prayer.

For people who are searching for the kingdom of love;
that they will accept the invitation God gives to everyone,
and have the courage
to follow the path which leads them there.

Silence

Lord, in your love:
Listen to our prayer.

For those who have died and are at peace with God;
that, welcomed into his heavenly kingdom of love,
they will enjoy eternal life and glory there.

Silence

Lord, in your love:
Listen to our prayer.

For people who have wandered away from God;
that, trusting in his gentle forgiveness and tender love,
they will choose to change their hearts and lives,
and take their rightful place in his kingdom.

Silence

Lord, in your love:
Listen to our prayer.

Knowing that our heavenly Father is listening,
in the silence of our hearts
let us share our own unspoken prayers with him.

Silence

Heavenly Father,
hear the prayers of your children,
and help us to follow you faithfully.
When we struggle,
help us always to choose your loving way,
so that we may belong to your kingdom.
We ask you to grant this through Jesus Christ our Lord.
Amen.

11
GOD'S WAY

Life is a journey, as we all make our way towards the promise of everlasting happiness in heaven. No two journeys are the same, and there are many things along the way which can make us change direction or pace. Sometimes we know what is expected of us, and we walk with confidence and joy. There are other times when we hesitate and falter, becoming distracted and maybe going the wrong way. There is someone who loves us and wants us to reach that final destination, where all will be well. Jesus said, 'I am the Way' (John 14:6). He came to show us how to find the right path which leads to eternal life. This path is not always easy to follow, and when we stumble and fall, or lose our sense of direction, he is ready to help us up and be our loving guide.

Thy will be done

As brothers and sisters in God's kingdom of love,
we ask our heavenly Father to listen
as we pray together:

For the Body of Christ, the Church, and her people;
may the Holy Spirit guide and lead all God's children
towards the kingdom of heaven.

Silence

Lord, in your mercy:
Show us your way.

For all who work to build God's kingdom on earth;
may the Holy Spirit guide and inspire them
to live by Christ's commandments
to love God and one another.

Silence

Lord, in your mercy:
Show us your way.

For nations and communities divided by conflict and fear;
may the Holy Spirit guide and strengthen them
to love their enemies,
to do good to those who hate them,
and to forgive rather than condemn.

Silence

Lord, in your mercy:
Show us your way.

For those who have lost their faith and their way in life;
may the Holy Spirit search for them
and lovingly guide them back to the path
which leads to eternal life.

Silence

Lord, in your mercy:
Show us your way.

For wisdom and understanding of God's way;
may the Holy Spirit guide us
and help us to accept that God's way
is often not the human way,
and that we must trust in his goodness.

Silence

Lord, in your mercy:
Show us your way.

Knowing that our heavenly Father is listening,
in the silence of our hearts
let us share our own unspoken prayers with him.

Silence

Heavenly Father,
as we follow the way of Christ,
keep us faithful to you
and forever close to your love and friendship.
We ask this through Christ your Son.
Amen.

The path to heaven

As we gather as one family,
united by faith and love,
let us turn to God with our prayers:

We pray for peace in our world;
that as Christians we will find a way to reconciliation
through forgiveness and love,
however difficult that path might be.

Silence

Lord, lead us:
Along your loving path.

We pray for understanding and acceptance in our world;
that as Christians we will find a way
to God's generosity of heart,
by welcoming and supporting
those who have wandered far from his path.

Silence

Lord, lead us:
Along your loving path.

We pray for those who strive for material wealth
above everything else;
that as Christians we will find a way
to show them by our daily lives
that it is more important to have treasure in heaven
than here on earth.

Silence

Lord, lead us:
Along your loving path.

We pray for people who suffer hardship or persecution
because of their faith;
that as Christians we will find a way
to uphold the rights of every person
to have the freedom to worship without fear.

Silence

Lord, lead us:
Along your loving path.

We pray for all who have died;
we give thanks that in life they have followed the way
which has led them to the peace and glory
of eternal life with God.

Silence

Lord, lead us:
Along your loving path.

Knowing that our heavenly Father is listening,
in the silence of our hearts
let us share our own unspoken prayers with him.

Silence

Loving Father,
as we make our way through life,
let us help one another to follow the path
which leads to your heavenly kingdom.
Grant this in the name of Christ our Lord.
Amen.

12
COMMANDMENTS OF LOVE

Without rules and regulations in our lives, everyone would do whatever they liked and it wouldn't take long for chaos to prevail. Without direction in our lives, we tend to wander aimlessly and are in danger of losing our way. In the Old Testament, God gave the Ten Commandments to his people, to help them to know the difference between right and wrong, and to live in his love and friendship. In the New Testament, Jesus gave us new commandments of love to complete the ones we already had. These are the foundation blocks on which we build our lives as his disciples today.

Jesus commanded us to love God and to love our neighbour as ourselves (Luke 10:27). But sometimes we might ask, 'Who exactly is my neighbour?' Every person created in the image and likeness of God is our neighbour. We are given the opportunity to do for others what we would like to do for God; to put our love into living action by loving every other human being. Jesus said, 'Whatever you do to the least of my brothers or sisters, you do to me.' (Matthew 25:40)

Love God and one another

Jesus said,
'When two or three gather together in my name,
I will be there with them.'
Let us ask God to listen now
as we bring our concerns and needs before him.

We pray for the Church throughout the world;
by our Christian love for God and our neighbour
may we lay the foundations for God's kingdom
in our daily lives.

Silence

Loving Father:
Grant our prayer.

We pray for those who suffer injustice,
exploitation and discrimination;
by our Christian love for God and our neighbour
may we take effective action against evil
and defend everyone's right to life.

Silence

Loving Father:
Grant our prayer.

We pray for nations and families
devastated by conflict and hatred;
by our Christian love for God and our neighbour
may our care and loving support for them
turn sadness to joy, hatred to forgiveness,
and bring the gift of God's peace to their lives.

Silence

Loving Father:
Grant our prayer.

We pray for those who are sick
and all who suffer in mind or body;
by our Christian love for God and our neighbour
may we discover the face of Christ
in those who are bruised by pain and suffering.

Silence

Loving Father:
Grant our prayer.

Knowing that our heavenly Father is listening,
in the silence of our hearts
let us share our own unspoken prayers with him.

Silence

Lord God,
we cannot love you unless we love one another.
Help us to become people of forgiveness and compassion
who recognise your face in the people we see around us.
We make our prayers through Christ our Lord.
Amen.

Love our neighbour

Jesus taught us to ask God for all our needs,
and, confident in his love, we gather together
to pray for all our brothers and sisters:

We pray for countries facing famine, flood, drought,
and any kind of disaster;
may we never pass by and ignore
the troubles of our neighbour,
but do everything we can to provide for all their needs.

Silence

Lord, help us:
To love one another.

We pray for the homeless and refugees
who have lost everything they own;
may we never turn away from our neighbour in need,
but respond with loving generosity and welcoming kindness.

Silence

Lord, help us:
To love one another.

We pray for those who are poor;
may our love enrich the lives of our neighbours,
and may our support for aid agencies
help to improve the quality of their care.

Silence

Lord, help us:
To love one another.

We pray for peace in our world;
may understanding and forgiveness
between neighbouring nations and religions
make our world a happy and hopeful place to live.

Silence

Lord, help us:
To love one another.

We pray for all who follow in the footsteps of Christ;
may we put our love for God and our neighbour
into action every day,
and bear living witness to our Christian love.

Silence

Lord, help us:
To love one another.

Knowing that our heavenly Father is listening,
in the silence of our hearts
let us share our own unspoken prayers with him.

Silence

Father,
may we be faithful to the name we bear
as followers of Christ.
Let your love make us worthy
to be called your sons and daughters.
Grant this through Christ our Lord.
Amen.

Love one another

As brothers and sisters in one loving family,
we ask God our Father to listen to our prayers:

We pray for people who are filled with hatred
and seek revenge;
help them to love their enemies of the past,
and to make them friends of the future.

Silence

Loving Father:
Hear our prayer.

We pray for the nations of the world;
may their governments and leaders
uphold the rights of their people,
and respect the value of every person.

Silence

Loving Father:
Hear our prayer.

We pray for people in any kind of need;
help us to love God by loving our neighbour
who is every person we meet.

Silence

Loving Father:
Hear our prayer.

We pray for those who feel unloved or alone;
may they be filled with hope and strength,
knowing that their heavenly Father loves the unloved,
searches for the lost,
and never abandons his children.

Silence

Loving Father:
Hear our prayer.

Knowing that our heavenly Father is listening,
in the silence of our hearts
let us share our own unspoken prayers with him.

Silence

God of tender love,
may our love for you and for one another
draw us closer to you and your heavenly kingdom.
Listen to these our prayers,
which we make in the name of Christ our Lord.
Amen.

13
LISTENING

In today's busy, noisy world it can be difficult to listen. There are many distractions and barriers which stop us from listening effectively and really understanding what is being said to us. In the same way, we find it annoying and difficult when others do not listen to what we have to say. Jesus understood the importance of listening well. He listened to his heavenly Father, who in turn listened to him when he made time to pray. We must listen carefully to the words of the Gospel, so that we can understand its message and what it means for us today in our daily lives.

Listen and live!

God does not turn away anyone
who comes to him asking for help.
Let us come before him now with open hearts
to pray for the needs of his people:

We pray for Christians as they worship all over the world;
that they will open their hearts and minds
to the Word of God,
and allow the love he reveals to fill their daily lives.

Silence

Heavenly Father:
Hear our prayer.

We pray for leaders of countries and governments;
that they will open their hearts and minds
to the Word of God,
and lead us by their example
to care for the poor and all those in need.

Silence

Heavenly Father:
Hear our prayer.

We pray for people whose hearts are hardened
by fear and hatred;
that they will open their hearts and minds
to the Word of God,
and allow its message of forgiveness and reconciliation
to fill their lives with peace.

Silence

Heavenly Father:
Hear our prayer.

We pray for ourselves and our communities;
that we will open our hearts and minds
to the Word of God,
and make time in our busy lives
to hear his voice as he speaks to us.

Silence

Heavenly Father:
Hear our prayer.

We pray for people who have no one to listen;
that they will open their hearts and minds
to the Word of God,
and understand that their heavenly Father
hears every word they speak and knows every thought they make.

Silence

Heavenly Father:
Hear our prayer.

Knowing that our heavenly Father is listening,
in the silence of our hearts
let us share our own unspoken prayers with him.

Silence

God our Father,
we know that you always listen to the prayers
of your people.
Help us to be people
who listen and understand your Word
which leads us to your heavenly kingdom.
We ask this in the name of Christ our Lord.
Amen.

14
MAKING CHOICES

Every day of our lives we have to make choices. Sometimes we make the wrong ones, and do something we later regret. When we realise our mistake and have a change of heart, God always forgives us and encourages us to carry on and try again. Jesus told many parables which told of our loving Father's forgiveness, but he also warned us about what would happen to those who ignore his words, and choose to follow their own foolish ways.

Choose God's way

As brothers and sisters in Christ,
let us gather together to ask our heavenly Father
to listen to the needs of his family:

Let us pray for our family, the Church;
may it choose to build itself on the rock
which is God's Word and Truth,
and live out Christ's Gospel of love for everyone.

Silence

Lord, hear us:
Help us to follow you.

Let us pray for the hungry, the homeless,
the stranger and the lonely;
may we choose to see the face of Christ
in every person we meet,
and treat him or her with kindness and respect.

Silence

Lord, hear us:
Help us to follow you.

We pray for people who are faced with difficult choices
in their lives;
may they choose to follow Christ's loving example,
and have the wisdom and courage
to follow the path along which he leads them.

Silence

Lord, hear us:
Help us to follow you.

Let us pray for peace in our world;
may people and countries choose to abandon hatred,

and set their hearts on returning to God's love
through forgiveness and reconciliation.

Silence

Lord, hear us:
Help us to follow you.

Let us pray for those who have died in faith;
may choosing to follow Christ in life
allow them to follow him in death
to the glory of his Father's heavenly kingdom.

Silence

Lord, hear us:
Help us to follow you.

Knowing that our heavenly Father is listening,
in the silence of our hearts
let us share our own unspoken prayers with him.

Silence

Heavenly Father,
may we choose to follow the example of the disciples
who walked in the footsteps of Christ.
Help us to make wise decisions in our lives,
and never to wander far from the path of your love.
We ask this through Christ our Lord.
Amen.

God chooses us

As children in one loving family of God,
we come before our heavenly Father
to ask for all our needs and concerns as we pray:

For Christians everywhere who are called to do God's will;
that they will choose to take up their cross every day
and follow Christ,
proclaiming his Good News to the world.

Silence

God of love:
May we do your will.

For agencies and organisations working for peace
in our troubled world;
that those they are trying to help
will choose to listen and respond
to the reconciliation and forgiveness they propose.

Silence

God of love:
May we do your will.

For people who campaign for justice and equal rights for all;
that they will choose non-violent and loving ways
to achieve an end to injustice and inequality.

Silence

God of love:
May we do your will.

For those who have turned away from God
and lost their way;
that they will choose to ask for his forgiveness
and renew their lives in his love.

Silence

God of love:
May we do your will.

For parents entrusted with the gift of new life;
that they will choose to nurture and protect their children,
and share God's gifts of faith and love.

Silence

God of love:
May we do your will.

Knowing that our heavenly Father is listening,
in the silence of our hearts
let us share our own unspoken prayers with him.

Silence

Loving Father,
hear the prayers of your family,
and answer them as we deserve.
Open our hearts to hear and understand your Holy Word,
so that we may always choose to do your will.
Grant this through Christ our Lord.
Amen.

15
TREASURE

Money and possessions do not make us rich in the sight of God. It does not matter how much we give, but what is in our hearts when we give. By living as Jesus taught us and sharing in God's kingdom now, we will store up treasure for ourselves in heaven. Every good deed or word of kindness is more precious to God than worldly riches can ever be. When we die, whatever money or possessions we have are left behind, but our goodness will last for ever and bring us everlasting happiness in the kingdom of heaven.

Riches in heaven

As God's children
we turn to our heavenly Father who loves us,
with all our troubles and cares:

Let us pray for the poor and the homeless;
may our loving care and concern enrich their lives,
as we do everything we can to ease their suffering and despair.

Silence

Caring Father:
Enrich our lives with love.

Let us pray for people who feel rejected or alone;
may a warm smile, a friendly word,
a caring visit or time spent listening
enrich their lonely lives.

Silence

Caring Father:
Enrich our lives with love.

Let us pray for people who believe
that money alone can bring happiness;
may their lives be enriched by the joy of sharing,
and by understanding that it is in giving that we truly receive.

Silence

Caring Father:
Enrich our lives with love.

Let us pray for love, forgiveness, generosity
and truth in our world;
may we understand what is important to God,
and not waste our lives on things that are worthless in heaven.

Silence

Caring Father:
Enrich our lives with love.

Knowing that our heavenly Father is listening,
in the silence of our hearts
let us share our own unspoken prayers with him.

Silence

Lord God,
in your loving kindness hear our prayers,
and help us to live as your sons and daughters,
as we build up your precious kingdom of love.
We make our prayers in the name of Jesus Christ our Lord.
Amen.

Rich and poor

Jesus said,
'When two or three gather together in my name,
I will be there with them.'
Let us ask God to listen now
as we bring our needs before him:

We pray for those who generously give up
their own comforts and luxuries
to help the poor, the homeless
and the unloved people in our world.

Silence

Lord of mercy:
Increase our love.

We pray that greed and selfishness
will not make us blind to the needs
of our brothers and sisters who are desperate for our help.

Silence

Lord of mercy:
Increase our love.

We pray that people who are forced to beg
or sleep on the streets
will meet Christ in our acts of kindness
and our respect for their human dignity.

Silence

Lord of mercy:
Increase our love.

We pray that our hearts will be filled with enough love
to make us ready to give our time, care, friendship and possessions
to anyone in need.

Silence

Lord of mercy:
Increase our love.

We pray that leaders and governments of rich countries
do not ignore the suffering of our brothers and sisters
who live in poor and underdeveloped parts of the world.

Silence

Lord of mercy:
Increase our love.

Knowing that our heavenly Father is listening,
in the silence of our hearts
let us share our own unspoken prayers with him.

Silence

Heavenly Father,
enrich the lives of those who are poor
and those who are wealthy,
by opening our eyes to see your living love
in the world around us.
Grant this through Christ our Lord.
Amen.

16
LITTLE CHILDREN

Jesus always made children feel welcome, and never turned them away. He recognised the importance and value of their childhood qualities of honesty, trust, unconditional love and forgiveness, and their straightforward and uncomplicated way of looking at life and seeing things. Jesus encourages us to keep these childhood qualities as we get older, so that as we grow in age and size, we may also grow closer to God and his kingdom of love.

Be like little children

In Baptism we are welcomed into the one family of God.
Let us come before God our loving Father
and pray for the needs of all our brothers and sisters worldwide:

We bring to God's love
all who teach the Christian faith by word and example;
we pray that God will work through them
to touch the hearts of all children
and bring them to know the joy of his gentle love.

Silence

Heavenly Father:
Listen to your children.

We bring to God's love
young children who are abused in mind or body;
we pray that God's healing power
will allow them to rebuild their lives
in homes and families filled with love
where fear has no place.

Silence

Heavenly Father:
Listen to your children.

We bring to God's love
the leaders of every country and nation;
we pray that they will defend the rights of young people
and protect children from exploitation and danger.

Silence

Heavenly Father:
Listen to your children.

We bring to God's love
the hungry and the poor;

we pray for those who must helplessly watch their children
as they suffer from lack of food or medical care.

Silence

Heavenly Father:
Listen to your children.

We bring to God's love
all newborn babies,
especially those who are unwanted or abandoned;
we pray for the agencies and services
which work to ensure that they find homes
where they will be loved and cherished.

Silence

Heavenly Father:
Listen to your children.

Knowing that our heavenly Father is listening,
in the silence of our hearts
let us share our own unspoken prayers with him.

Silence

Loving Father,
watch over all your children
and protect them from every harm.
May their innocence and trust
keep them forever close to you.
Grant this in the name of Christ our Lord.
Amen.

17
THE GOOD SHEPHERD

In Christ's time, a shepherd's job was to find food for his sheep and to protect them from wild animals. Often he had to travel long distances with his flock, searching for water and good pasture. At night he would gather his sheep into a pen or fold, and then lie across the entrance to make a 'gate'. Jesus compared his care for us with the care shown by a good shepherd who takes care of his flock. He knows each one of us by name and we know him, and, recognising his call, we are happy to follow wherever he might lead us.

The Shepherd and his flock

As brothers and sisters in God's kingdom of love,
we ask our heavenly Father
to listen to the prayers of his children, as we pray:

For the Church and its many Christian folds;
that we may be united as one flock
which listens to the voice of the Good Shepherd
and faithfully follows the one who guides and leads us
to the kingdom of love.

Silence

Loving Shepherd:
We want to follow you.

For peace in our troubled world:
that we may follow the example of the Good Shepherd
and always try to turn hatred to love,
and anger to understanding,
by using our gifts and talents
to build bridges of friendship between our neighbours.

Silence

Loving Shepherd:
We want to follow you.

For people who are suffering in any way;
that they may find comfort and hope
in knowing that the Good Shepherd and his followers
will help to care for them and protect them from harm.

Silence

Loving Shepherd:
We want to follow you.

For those who have died;
that they may be filled with the joy of everlasting life
as the Good Shepherd leads them to rest in eternal peace.

Silence

Loving Shepherd:
We want to follow you.

Knowing that our heavenly Father is listening,
in the silence of our hearts
let us share our own unspoken prayers with him.

Silence

Loving Father,
the Good Shepherd gave up his life
so that we might live for ever.
Open our ears and our hearts
to hear and understand his words,
and make us always ready
to follow wherever he might lead.
Grant this through Christ your Son.
Amen.

The loving Shepherd

With love in our hearts for God and one another,
let us pray for the needs of our world:

Christ the Good Shepherd calls us to follow him;
let us pray that Christians everywhere will listen to his voice
and answer his call to follow him faithfully.

Silence

Lord, hear us:
And lead us in love.

Christ the Good Shepherd gave up his life for us;
let us pray for all those who have suffered and died
for the sake of their faith.

Silence

Lord, hear us:
And lead us in love.

Christ the Good Shepherd knows each of us by name;
let us pray for people who feel alone and unloved in our world,
that through our actions and words
Christ's love for them will change their lives.

Lord, hear us:
And lead us in love.

Christ the Good Shepherd protects us from harm;
let us pray for people who are endangered by war, violence and hatred, that with our help and support they will find the path which leads to peace and happiness.

Silence

Lord, hear us:
And lead us in love.

Knowing that our heavenly Father is listening,
in the silence of our hearts
let us share our own unspoken prayers with him.

Silence

Heavenly Father,
listen to the prayers
of the faithful flock gathered here before you.
United in love, may we place all our trust and hope
in the loving Saviour who leads us to you.
We ask this through Christ our Lord.
Amen.

18
PRAYER

Jesus often set aside time to spend in the company of his heavenly Father through prayer. There are many different ways to pray, and words are not always necessary. Sometimes we can simply sit quietly and use our imagination or thoughts to pray; we might find that singing or listening to a beautiful piece of music is a very powerful way to pray. Whatever method we choose to use, to sit still and feel that God is very close and listening to us fills us with joy and a very special sense of peace.

Our Father

As one loving family we come together to pray,
knowing that our Father in heaven will listen to us
and answer when we call:

Let us pray for God's Church throughout the world;
may we bless our Father's holy name
and, by our love for him and one another,
allow his kingdom to grow.

Silence

God our Father:
Hear our prayer.

Let us pray for the leaders of governments and nations;
may their minds and hearts be guided
so that God's will is done
and all people may live in lasting peace and true freedom.

Silence

God our Father:
Hear our prayer.

Let us pray for peace and reconciliation in our lives;
may we forgive others as God forgives us,
and allow love to help us to make friends rather than enemies.

Silence

God our Father:
Hear our prayer.

Let us pray for the sick, the sad
and all who suffer in mind or body;
may God give them the strength they need
to cope with their pain,
and deliver them from every trouble and worry.

Silence

God our Father:
Hear our prayer.

Let us pray for one another;
may we make time in our daily lives
to draw closer to God through prayer,
and together grow in faith and love.

Silence

God our Father:
Hear our prayer.

Knowing that our heavenly Father is listening,
in the silence of our hearts
let us share our own unspoken prayers with him.

Silence

Father in heaven,
who knows and loves us so well,
listen to the prayers of your children
and help us to grow each day
in the image of your perfect Son.
We make these prayers through Christ our Lord.
Amen.

PART THREE

Following Jesus

19
COME, FOLLOW ME!

Jesus invites us to follow him as we make our way through life. Sometimes the path along which he leads is not easy to follow, and we can lose sight of where we are going and wander away. With his loving help and the encouragement of our brothers and sisters, we shall eventually reach our destination, which is heaven. As we get to know Jesus better on our journey, together we can share his love for the world, and, in our own way, call others to come and follow.

Walking with Jesus

As children of God,
we turn to our heavenly Father
with all our needs and concerns:

We pray for the Church;
as she leads her holy people,
may she walk humbly with Jesus,
allowing him to guide and direct her steps along the way.

Silence

Lord, in your love:
Walk beside us.

We pray for all who are filled with uncertainty and doubt;
as they make their journey through life,
may they walk faithfully with Jesus,
allowing him to take their hand
and be their friend and guide.

Silence

Lord, in your love:
Walk beside us.

We pray for those who are called to follow you
in the religious life;
as they dedicate their lives to obeying your will,
may they walk joyfully with Jesus,
allowing him to share the gift of his peace.

Silence

Lord, in your love:
Walk beside us.

We pray for people who are dying;
as their journey through life draws to a close,

may they walk confidently with Jesus
as he lovingly leads them
to God's kingdom of eternal life and peace.

Silence

Lord, in your love:
Walk beside us.

Knowing that our heavenly Father is listening,
in the silence of our hearts
let us share our own unspoken prayers with him.

Silence

God of patient love,
hear our prayers,
and give us the courage to follow
when we hear you call.
If we lose our way,
guide us back to the path
which leads to your heavenly kingdom.
We ask this in the name of Christ our Lord.
Amen.

Courage to follow

As brothers and sisters in Christ,
let us ask our loving Father
to hear the prayers of his children:

For the courage to follow Christ
and bear witness to his Gospel
by sharing his love and forgiveness with the world.

Silence

Lord, hear us:
And answer our prayer.

For the courage to follow Christ
when it means standing up for what is right,
and protecting the weak and defenceless.

Silence

Lord, hear us:
And answer our prayer.

For the courage to follow Christ
when we hear him calling us,
and to serve him in whatever way he asks of us.

Silence

Lord, hear us:
And answer our prayer.

For the courage to follow Christ
when others laugh at us and poke fun
because of what we believe.

Silence

Lord, hear us:
And answer our prayer.

For the courage to follow Christ
when we feel uncertain about which path to take
at difficult times of our lives.

Silence

Lord, hear us:
And answer our prayer.

Knowing that our heavenly Father is listening,
in the silence of our hearts
let us share our own unspoken prayers with him.

Silence

Loving Father,
send your Spirit of courage,
so that we may be your witnesses to the world,
as we follow your way of love.
We ask this in the name of Jesus
who is Lord for ever and ever.
Amen.

20
JESUS OUR FRIEND

True friendship takes time to grow and develop. We know that we are friends with someone when we can trust that person to share our dreams and feelings, and forgive us when we make a mistake. Friendship means spending time with one another, sharing our lives and listening to what the other has to say. Jesus is our perfect friend. His friendship changes the lives of everyone who is touched by his love, forgiveness and gentleness.

Friend to all

We pray to God our loving Father
with simple trust and humble hope,
bringing before him all our needs:

We pray for friendship in the Church
and among all her people;
as we devote our lives
to bringing the values of God's kingdom into the world,
may we share the gift of friendship
with our neighbours of every race, colour and religion.

Silence

Father of friendship:
Fill our lives with love.

We pray for friendship in our homes and families;
as we grow together in love and respect,
may we also grow in understanding
about what it means to share the friendship of Christ
by judging no one
and touching the lives of one another
with love and understanding.

Silence

Father of friendship:
Fill our lives with love.

We pray for greater friendship to be shown towards the poor,
the homeless and those who are outcasts;
as we follow in the footsteps of Christ,
may our actions and words
show the compassionate friendship of Christ
who saw no one as being beyond the reach of God's grace
or his message of love and forgiveness.

Silence

Father of friendship:
Fill our lives with love.

We pray for friendship
between the nations and religions of the world;
As children of God
may we respect and accept our neighbours far and near,
forgiving past mistakes
and striving to fill our world with peace and understanding.

Silence

Father of friendship:
Fill our lives with love.

Knowing that our heavenly Father is listening,
in the silence of our hearts
let us share our own unspoken prayers with him.

Silence

Father, may your loving friendship
guide our daily lives.
By knowing and loving you
may we know and love our neighbour,
and become a friend to everyone we meet.
We ask this through Christ our Lord.
Amen.

Forgiving friend

My brothers and sisters,
let us bring our needs to God
and humbly ask him to hear our prayers:

Let us pray for the Church, the Body of Christ;
that it will not be bound by narrow-mindedness,
and will reach out to welcome
all who need Christ's healing love.

Silence

Forgiving Father:
Open our hearts.

Let us pray for countries and people
devastated by war and hatred;
that, trusting in God's merciful love,
they will be able to open their hearts and lives
to allow forgiveness and reconciliation
to become the foundation stones
on which they build new friendships.

Silence

Forgiving Father:
Open our hearts.

Let us pray for anyone in need of forgiveness and healing;
that they will have the courage to admit their mistakes,
and, by changing their hearts and lives,
put right what they have done wrong,
and begin a new life of friendship with God.

Silence

Forgiving Father:
Open our hearts.

Let us pray for parents and children everywhere;
that our homes and families
will be places where we learn to forgive and be forgiven,
and to celebrate the peace and joy
that reconciliation with God and one another brings.

Silence

Forgiving Father:
Open our hearts.

Knowing that our heavenly Father is listening,
in the silence of our hearts
let us share our own unspoken prayers with him.

Silence

Lord God,
Jesus came to be a friend to all;
to forgive the unforgiving,
to love the unloved,
and to change the lives of those he healed.
May we try every day to become more like him,
and to deepen our friendship
with you and each other.
Grant this in the name of Christ your Son.
Amen.

21
WELCOME

Everyone likes to feel welcome and to be treated kindly. Jesus shares his love with anyone who makes him welcome. He told us: 'Whatever you do to others you do to me' (Matthew 25:40). When we treat other people with love and kindness, and make them feel welcome at home, at school or at any time in our everyday lives, then we are doing the same to Jesus.

A warm welcome

United in love,
we gather as brothers and sisters
to pray for our own needs and the needs of the world:

We pray for the Church and all her people;
that we may warmly welcome fellow Christians,
and, in mutual love and respect,
we may grow in understanding and unity.

Silence

Merciful Father:
Hear our prayer.

We pray for all who work to spread the Good News;
that they may share the peace of Christ
with everyone who makes them welcome.

Silence

Merciful Father:
Hear our prayer.

We pray for refugees and all who are driven from their homes
by war or disaster;
that we may welcome them warmly
and reach out the hand of friendship at their time of need.

Silence

Merciful Father:
Hear our prayer.

We pray for the homeless
and anyone who has fallen on hard times;
that we may always recognise the image of Christ in their faces
and never walk by and ignore their cries for help.

Silence

Merciful Father:
Hear our prayer.

We pray for the families worshipping here today;
that, by celebrating this Eucharist together,
we may make time to welcome Jesus and one another,
and share the gifts of his love and joy.

Silence

Merciful Father:
Hear our prayer.

Knowing that our heavenly Father is listening,
in the silence of our hearts
let us share our own unspoken prayers with him.

Silence

Heavenly Father,
may we see you in the people around us,
and always welcome you
with a warm smile and a loving heart.
We ask this through Christ our Lord.
Amen.

22
JOURNEY

From the moment we are born, we each begin our own special journey through life. Along the way we meet many different people who touch our lives with their love and help us along the way. We cannot help wondering about God and what he wants for us and expects from us. We want to find out more about him, to try to stay close to him, and discover how we can serve him in our ordinary everyday lives. We cheerfully put up with the journey when the going is tough, because there is something and someone to look forward to at the end of it. Finally, in heaven, we will find the peace, joy and happiness we have been promised.

Journey of discovery

United in love,
we gather as brothers and sisters in Christ
to pray for our own needs and the needs of the world:

We pray for the Church and all Christian people;
on our journey through life
may we be guided by the light of faith
towards Christ our Saviour,
just as the wise men were guided by the light of a star.

Silence

Loving Father:
Lead us.

We pray for all who proclaim the Good News to the world
by words and deeds;
may the Holy Spirit guide us on our journey through life
as we share our faith with the world
and enjoy the peace of God's kingdom.

Silence
Loving Father:
Lead us.

We pray for people forced to leave their homes and families
because of war, fear or disaster;
may they be guided on their journey of uncertainty and suffering
by our loving support and efforts to bring them comfort and hope.

Silence

Loving Father:
Lead us.

We pray for people wandering in the wilderness of doubt
as they search for God in their lives;

may our loving Father who searches for everyone who is lost
guide them on their journey of discovery.

Silence

Loving Father:
Lead us.

We pray for anyone who has wandered far from God's love;
may they be guided on a journey of friendship and reconciliation,
as they discover the forgiveness and healing
of our heavenly Father who never stops loving them.

Silence

Loving Father:
Lead us.

Knowing that our heavenly Father is listening,
in the silence of our hearts
let us share our own unspoken prayers with him.

Silence

Heavenly Father,
as we journey through life,
keep us close to your love
and mould us in the image of Christ your loving Son.
We ask this in the name of Jesus our Lord.
Amen.

Journey of joy

Because we are so very precious to God,
he takes care of us and listens tenderly
to all our worries and concerns, as we pray:

For those who are preparing for Baptism
and to become members of the Church;
may we welcome them as Christ was welcomed into Jerusalem,
and together celebrate and share their joyful journey of faith.

Silence

Lord, hear us:
And grant our prayer.

For mothers and families awaiting the birth of a child;
may we share their joy and happiness,
and, like Mary the mother of Jesus,
proclaim God's infinite love and greatness to the world.

Silence

Lord, hear us:
And grant our prayer.

For an end to hatred, cruelty and violence in our world;
may forgiveness and reconciliation
allow people to share the joyful journey towards lasting peace.

Silence

Lord, hear us:
And grant our prayer.

For people who have lost contact with family and friends;
may they never give up hope of being joyfully reunited in love.

Silence

Lord, hear us:
And grant our prayer.

For those who have completed their journey through life;
may they share in the glory of Christ's resurrection
and the joy of eternal life.

Silence

Lord, hear us:
And grant our prayer.

Knowing that our heavenly Father is listening,
in the silence of our hearts
let us share our own unspoken prayers with him.

Silence

God our Father,
hear the prayers of your children
gathered here before you.
As we journey towards your heavenly kingdom,
fill us with the joy of your love
which we share with one another.
We ask this through Christ our Lord.
Amen.

Everyday journeys

As sons and daughters of God our Father,
we come together to pray:

Let us pray for people who are on a personal journey of faith;
may they discover a community of faith
which welcomes and inspires them
by our Christian example.

Silence

Lord, hear our prayer:
And guide your loving people.

Let us pray for governments and nations
taking the first steps on the journey towards peace;
may forgiveness and understanding
lead them along the path towards reconciliation and friendship.

Silence

Lord, hear our prayer:
And guide your loving people.

Let us pray for refugees
forced to journey far from their homes;
may our support for those who work to relieve their suffering
help to bring them comfort and hope.

Silence

Lord, hear our prayer:
And guide your loving people.

Let us pray for young people
as they make the journey from childhood to adulthood;
may they have the courage
to face all the new challenges they meet along the way,
and the strength and faith to stay close to God's love.

Silence

Lord, hear our prayer:
And guide your loving people.

Let us pray for all travellers today;
may they meet no danger on their journeys,
and arrive safely wherever they are going.

Silence

Lord, hear our prayer:
And guide your loving people.

Knowing that our heavenly Father is listening,
in the silence of our hearts
let us share our own unspoken prayers with him.

Silence

Lord God,
watch over your beloved children
as we make our daily journey through life.
Keep us ever close to your love,
so that we may be your witnesses to the world.
Grant this in the name of Christ your only Son.
Amen.

23
KEEP YOURSELVES READY!

When we know that something is about to happen we can prepare ourselves so that it does not take us by surprise. We know that Jesus will return at the end of time, but only God the Father knows exactly when that will be. So Jesus urges us to keep ourselves ready by obeying his commandments and trying to follow his loving way every day of our lives.

Be prepared

Trusting in God's merciful love for us,
we come before him with our prayers:

We bring to God's love the family gathered here today
and our brothers and sisters throughout the world;
we pray that by following Christ
and leading lives of love, forgiveness and truth,
he will find us ready to greet him whenever he returns.

Silence

Loving Lord:
Hear our prayer.

We bring to God's love the homeless, the poor and the unloved;
we pray that we will generously share what we have with others,
and reach out a helping hand of friendship to all in need.

Loving Lord:
Hear our prayer.

We bring to God's forgiving love those who hate
and are filled with anger;
we pray that we will share the gift of Christ's peace with the world,
and melt their hardened hearts with love and forgiveness.

Silence

Loving Lord:
Hear our prayer.

We bring to God's healing love those who are sick and suffering;
we pray that our loving care and concern
will help to bring them closer to God
and give them fresh strength and hope.

Silence

Loving Lord:
Hear our prayer.

We bring to God's tender love our ordinary everyday lives;
we pray that we will see and hear Christ
in the people and the world around us,
and always try to make each day pleasing in his sight.

Silence

Loving Lord:
Hear our prayer.

Knowing that our heavenly Father is listening,
in the silence of our hearts
let us share our own unspoken prayers with him.

Silence

Almighty God,
listen to our prayers
and answer them in your own loving way.
Keep us close to your love
and ready to greet Christ when he returns in glory.
We ask this in the name of Christ our Lord.
Amen.

24
HAVE COURAGE

It is not easy to be a follower of Jesus and take our place in society as a Christian. Jesus warned his disciples that they would need courage and strength for their mission of sharing the Good News with the world; indeed, many of them were put to death for their faith. Jesus himself experienced great fear as he prayed in the Garden of Gethsemane before being led away to suffer and die.

He reassures us that we will never be alone at times of fear; he is always beside us to share our troubles. The gifts of the Holy Spirit will fill us with the courage and strength we need to share our faith with the world, and to build God's kingdom on earth.

Do not be afraid

God created us in his own image to be like him.
Let us turn to him with our prayers for one another:

We pray for the Church and all her people;
may the Spirit of courage help each of us
to be a witness to Christ's love in our everyday lives.

Silence

Almighty God:
Make us strong.

We pray for people who are persecuted and imprisoned
for the sake of their religion;
may the Spirit of courage give them the strength
to forgive their enemies
and give us the determination to work for their freedom.

Silence

Almighty God:
Make us strong.

We pray for the sick and anyone who is suffering;
may the Spirit of courage help them to face their pain
and bring them his healing peace.

Silence

Almighty God:
Make us strong.

We pray for ourselves and the family gathered here today;
may the Spirit of courage guide our words
and help us to speak with wisdom and understanding,
so that others may know and love Christ our Lord.

Silence

Almighty God:
Make us strong.

Knowing that our heavenly Father is listening,
in the silence of our hearts
let us share our own unspoken prayers with him.

Silence

Loving Father,
as we share the work of Christ your Son,
help us to bring Good News to the poor,
liberty to captives,
sight to the blind,
and freedom to the downtrodden.
Grant these prayers through Christ your Son.
Amen.

25
MISSION

Jesus had a mission to reveal God's love to the world and to save us from sin. From the beginning of his public preaching, he appointed apostles from among his followers, and sent them out in his name to preach the Gospel. Jesus said, 'As the Father has sent me, so I send you' (John 20:21), and he gave them the authority and power to share the Good News with the entire human race. The mission of Jesus and his followers is continued today through the Church and all Christians, under the guidance of the Holy Spirit.

Go out to the world

United in love,
we gather as brothers and sisters
to pray for our own needs and the needs of others:

We pray for the Church
and her mission to live and share the Gospel;
may we each play our part
in revealing God's love to the world.

Silence

Lord, we ask you:
Hear our prayer.

We pray for understanding and dialogue
among the Christian Churches;
may we work together and pray for the gift of perfect unity.

Silence

Lord, we ask you:
Hear our prayer.

We pray for courage to be witnesses for Christ;
may the gifts of the Holy Spirit
help us never to be afraid to proclaim our faith
by our words and actions.

Silence

Lord, we ask you:
Hear our prayer.

We pray for people who dedicate their lives
to missionary work;
may God protect them from danger
as they share his kingdom with the world.

Silence

Lord, we ask you:
Hear our prayer.

Knowing that our heavenly Father is listening,
in the silence of our hearts
let us share our own unspoken prayers with him.

Silence

Almighty God,
you sent Christ your Son to be our Saviour.
May we your people carry on his mission
to share his salvation with the world.
We ask this through Christ our Lord,
who reigns with you for ever and ever.
Amen.

Share the Good News

By our Baptism we belong to the one family of God.
Let us pray now for that family:

That the Word of God will unite all of God's people
in forgiveness and love for one another.

Silence

We pray to the Lord:
Lord, hear our prayer.

That the Word of God will take root
in hearts hardened by hatred
and change them into loving hearts
where God's peace can find a home.

Silence

We pray to the Lord:
Lord, hear our prayer.

That the Word of God will bring hope to the poor
and comfort to all who are burdened
by troubles and fears.

Silence

We pray to the Lord:
Lord, hear our prayer.

That the Word of God will enliven our faith
and fill us with joy,
knowing how much our Father loves his children.

Silence

We pray to the Lord:
Lord, hear our prayer.

That the Word of God will grow
and bear fruit in our lives
as each day we try to live the Gospel
and its message of unconditional love for everyone.

Silence

We pray to the Lord:
Lord, hear our prayer.

Knowing that our heavenly Father is listening,
in the silence of our hearts
let us share our own unspoken prayers with him.

Silence

Father of all,
you revealed yourself to the world
through Christ our Saviour,
the Word made flesh,
who lived as a man among us.
May the Holy Spirit open our minds
to understand your living Word today.
We make this and all our prayers
through Christ our Lord.
Amen.

26
WITNESS

When someone is described as being a 'witness', it means that they were present at some event or happening which they can give evidence or a visual account of. They are able to testify or declare what happened on a particular occasion. Christ had many such witnesses, including John the Baptist, his disciples, and everyone who saw and heard the wonderful things he did and said. Many of these things are written down in the New Testament and passed down faithfully, so that we in turn can be witnesses to Jesus Christ and God's love for the world.

Witnesses for the world

We come before our heavenly Father
to ask him to listen lovingly
to the prayers of his children:

We bring to our Father's love
his people and his Church;
may he give us the courage and strength
to be his witnesses,
so that through us many others may know
and believe in him.

Silence

Hear us, Father:
And send your Spirit.

We bring to our Father's love
those who are imprisoned
or made to suffer for their beliefs;
by their faithful witness to his truth and love,
may they be filled with joy and happiness,
knowing that their names will be written for ever in heaven.

Silence

Hear us, Father:
And send your Spirit.

We bring to our Father's love
the homeless, the unemployed and the downhearted;
may he give us the compassion and understanding
to witness to his love by reaching out in friendship
to help anyone in need. to those in need.

Silence

Hear us, Father:
And send your Spirit.

We bring to our Father's love
all who are called to the missionary life;
as they go out to a world filled with doubt
and bear witness to the Gospel of love and forgiveness,
may our prayers and support bring them comfort and joy.

Silence

Hear us, Father:
And send your Spirit.

We bring to our Father's love
all who have died;
after lives of faithful service
may they now be witnesses to the peace and joy
of God's glorious kingdom in heaven.

Silence

Hear us, Father:
And send your Spirit.

Knowing that our heavenly Father is listening,
in the silence of our hearts
let us share our own unspoken prayers with him.

Silence

Lord God,
Christ your Son came as your witness
so that we might know and love you.
Send us out into the world
to share your message of peace and eternal life.
Grant this through Christ your Son.
Amen.

27
GOOD NEWS

'Good News' is the modern English equivalent of the Anglo-Saxon word 'godspell'. The Gospels which make up the New Testament proclaim the Good News that God's plan for the world has been carried out and successfully completed by Jesus Christ. The Good News shares the message of God's love with all of humanity. Everyone can have a piece of that Good News for themselves.

Hear the Good News

We have heard the Good News
and understood its message.
Now we ask our heavenly Father to listen to our prayers
for the Church and the world:

We pray for the Church of Christ
and its mission to the world;
may we have courage as followers of Christ
to answer his call to proclaim the Good News
in our homes, our schools and our everyday lives.

Silence

God our Father:
Hear our prayer.

We pray for all Christians who are imprisoned
or persecuted because of their faith;
may we be inspired by their brave example
and support them with our love and prayers.

Silence

God our Father:
Hear our prayer.

We pray for people who have heard the Good News
but are filled with doubt and uncertainty;
may God's Word take root in their hearts and minds
through understanding,
and allow its seeds of love and faith to grow
and produce a rich harvest.

Silence

God our Father:
Hear our prayer.

We pray for peacemakers
and all who hold positions of authority throughout our world;
may the Gospel message help them to heal old wounds
between nations and religions,
and lead us to open our hearts
to forgiveness and reconciliation.

Silence

God our Father:
Hear our prayer.

We pray for the family gathered here today;
may we respond to the Gospel
which calls us to serve one another,
and not become blind to the needs of the people around us.

Silence

God our Father:
Hear our prayer.

Knowing that our heavenly Father is listening,
in the silence of our hearts
let us share our own unspoken prayers with him.

Silence

Father in heaven,
help us to listen to and understand the Good News,
so that we can joyfully proclaim
and share it with the world.
Grant this and all our prayers through Christ our Lord.
Amen.

28
BAPTISM

In Baptism we become sons and daughters of God our Father, and the brothers and sisters of one another. As God's children we are called by name to belong to one family, the Christian Church. God gives us the gift of the Holy Spirit to fill us with his life and love, and to help us to grow in faith and understanding as we share the Gospel message of love throughout our lives.

New life in the Spirit

We come before the Father in love
to ask him to listen to our prayers:

Christ came to proclaim the Good News to the world;
filled with the Holy Spirit,
may we as Christians share his mission and Gospel
with enthusiasm and joy.

Silence

Lord of life:
Fill us with your Spirit.

Christ came to lead us away from sin;
filled with the Holy Spirit,
may we turn back to God and his loving ways
with readiness to forgive others as we are forgiven.

Silence

Lord of life:
Fill us with your Spirit.

Christ came to show us the way to God's kingdom;
filled with the Holy Spirit,
may we have the courage to follow him
and help others who share our journey along the way.

Silence

Lord of life:
Fill us with your Spirit.

Christ came to share his life and love;
filled with the Holy Spirit,
may the water of life become a spring within us
and flow out into our daily lives
as words and actions which are filled with love.

Silence

Lord of life:
Fill us with your Spirit.

Christ came to heal the sick and raise the dead to life;
filled with the Holy Spirit,
may the suffering and the dying be comforted by his peace
and the promise of eternal life and happiness
in God's heavenly kingdom.

Silence

Lord of life:
Fill us with your Spirit.

Knowing that our heavenly Father is listening,
in the silence of our hearts
let us share our own unspoken prayers with him.

Silence

Lord God,
through Baptism we are reborn
to new life as your children.
Filled with your living Spirit,
may we share your salvation and joy
with the whole world.
Grant this in the name of Christ our Lord.
Amen.

Come, Holy Spirit

Gathered together in love,
as brothers and sisters in Christ,
let us ask our loving Father to listen to the prayers we make:

We pray for all God's people;
that through Baptism we may be filled with the Holy Spirit
and remain faithful to our calling as children of God.

Silence

Heavenly Father:
Hear our prayer.

We pray for all who are preparing to be baptised;
that our prayers may help them to accept joyfully
the outpouring of the Holy Spirit and his many gifts.

Silence

Heavenly Father:
Hear our prayer.

We pray for all who have died;
that they will rise to the new and everlasting life
promised through their Baptism in Christ.

Silence

Heavenly Father:
Hear our prayer.

We pray for the sick and all who suffer;
that the Holy Spirit living within them
will bring them healing and peace.

Silence

Heavenly Father:
Hear our prayer.

We pray for the families gathered here today;
that God will pour out his Holy Spirit to strengthen us
and to be our helper and guide today and every day.

Silence

Heavenly Father:
Hear our prayer.

Knowing that our heavenly Father is listening,
in the silence of our hearts
let us share our own unspoken prayers with him.

Silence

Father,
by water and the Spirit
you free us from sin and give us new life.
May your Spirit living in us
help us to become more like Christ
your beloved Son.
Grant this through Jesus our Lord.
Amen.

29
SON OF GOD

Jesus is the only beloved Son of God, who revealed the nature of his heavenly Father who would otherwise remain a mystery to the world. He taught us to call God 'Our Father' and told us: 'Anyone who has seen me has seen the Father' (John 13:9). Jesus, in his words, actions and attitudes, reveals to us in a very human way what God is like; for he is both God and man. Jesus came to fulfil his Father's plan to save the world, and to share the gift of eternal life with all people.

We believe

As brothers and sisters in Baptism,
let us gather together to ask our heavenly Father
to listen to the needs of his family everywhere:

We bring before God the Church and all her people;
may our Christian lives reveal Christ's face to the world,
so that others may know and believe in him.

Silence

Lord, hear us:
And answer our prayer.

We bring before God
those who are blinded by doubt and uncertainty;
may their hearts and minds be opened
to see God's love in the people around them,
so that they may believe in him.

Silence

Lord, hear us:
And answer our prayer.

We bring before God
those who are preparing to be baptised
and received into the Christian Church;
may they grow strong in faith
and become loving witnesses to the God they believe in.

Silence

Lord, hear us:
And answer our prayer.

We bring before God
all who are persecuted or made to suffer
because they are Christians;

may they find the strength and courage to stand firm
when challenged by hatred and prejudice.

Silence

Lord, hear us:
And answer our prayer.

We bring before God the lives of this family of faith;
may we be given the hands of Christ to work with,
the heart of Christ to love with,
and the mind of Christ to enlighten the world.

Silence

Lord, hear us:
And answer our prayer.

Knowing that our heavenly Father is listening,
in the silence of our hearts
let us share our own unspoken prayers with him.

Silence

God our Father,
Christ your Son revealed the depth
of your love and forgiveness for the world.
Increase our faith and love,
so that we may share your life and kingdom with others.
We ask this in the name of Christ our Lord.
Amen.

PART FOUR

God supplies our needs

30
HEALING

Nothing is impossible for God! Jesus worked many miracles in his Father's name, transforming the lives of all sorts of people with his power. By healing those who believed in him, he revealed that he was indeed the Son of God who had come to bring the Good News to the whole world. He takes pity on everyone who asks for his help, and his compassionate healing and tender love bring immeasurable joy and hope to many lives.

Heal our lives

As we gather as one family,
united by faith and love,
let us turn to God with our prayers:

We pray for Christians everywhere;
may the differences which divide our communities
be healed by the love we share for God and one another.

Silence

Almighty God:
Heal our lives.

We pray for people whose homes and livelihoods
have been destroyed by disaster;
may our efforts to relieve their suffering
help to heal their broken lives.

Silence

Almighty God:
Heal our lives.

We pray for peace in our homes and our world;
may our understanding and forgiveness
heal wounds of conflict and tension.

Silence

Almighty God:
Heal our lives.

We pray for the sick and all who suffer;
may the power of God's healing love
touch their lives and fill them with strength and hope.

Silence

Almighty God:
Heal our lives.

Knowing that our heavenly Father is listening,
in the silence of our hearts
let us share our own unspoken prayers with him.

Silence

Loving Father,
hear the prayers of your children
and touch our lives with your healing love.
May our faith in you continue to grow ever stronger,
changing our lives
and making them ever more pleasing to you.
We ask this in the name
of Jesus Christ our Lord.
Amen.

Change our lives

God has the power to change our lives.
Trusting in his fatherly love,
we ask him to listen to our needs and the needs of others:

Jesus gave sight to blind people;
we pray that many lives will be changed
when we help each other to see and recognise Christ
in the people and the world around us.

Silence

Listen, Lord:
And change our lives.

Jesus made disabled people walk;
we pray that many lives will be changed
when people ask Jesus to walk beside them
and be their loving guide through life.

Silence

Listen, Lord:
And change our lives.

Jesus gave voices to those who could not speak;
we pray that the lives of many will be changed
when they hear and speak the Word of God
and share its message of love for all.

Silence

Listen, Lord:
And change our lives.

Jesus made lepers welcome;
we pray that many lives will be changed
by our attitudes of loving friendship and acceptance
towards all who are rejected by society
because of disability, illness or disfigurement.

Silence

Listen, Lord:
And change our lives.

Knowing that our heavenly Father is listening,
in the silence of our hearts
let us share our own unspoken prayers with him.

Silence

Almighty God,
you have the power to change our lives
if we allow you.
May we try to become more and more
like Christ your Son,
whose love changed our world for ever.
Grant this through Jesus our Lord.
Amen.

31
FORGIVENESS

God loves us so much that he forgives all our mistakes. Lovingly he watches and waits, hoping that when we choose to wander away from his love, we will one day turn back to him, longing for forgiveness and full of determination to make a fresh start. God's love for us is so great that he sent his only Son Jesus to be our Saviour and rescue us from our sins. Just as we are forgiven, in the same way God expects us to show the same forgiveness and mercy to others.

Lord of forgiveness

Trusting in God's merciful love for us,
we come before him with our prayers:

We bring to God's forgiving love
his Church and his people;
we pray that people who have turned away from him
may rediscover the path which leads to his love.

Silence

Lord of forgiveness:
Lead us back to your love.

We bring to God's forgiving love
nations and people who are divided by hatred and conflict;
we pray that the power of his love
will make us forgiving towards one another,
just as he is forgiving towards us.

Silence

Lord of forgiveness:
Lead us back to your love.

We bring to God's forgiving love
people in prison and the families who suffer with them;
we pray that as Christians
we may offer compassion instead of judgement,
and give them the opportunity
to leave their mistakes in the past and make a fresh start.

Silence

Lord of forgiveness:
Lead us back to your love.

We bring to God's forgiving love
those whose hearts and lives

are so filled with resentment and anger
that there is little room for forgiveness;
we pray that he will heal their hardened hearts
and transform their lives with love.

Silence

Lord of forgiveness:
Lead us back to your love.

Knowing that our heavenly Father is listening,
in the silence of our hearts
let us share our own unspoken prayers with him.

Silence

Forgiving Father,
you are full of mercy and compassion;
mould us in your image,
and help us to become people of forgiveness,
so that we may grow closer to you.
Grant this through Christ our Lord.
Amen.

Change our hearts

God loved the world so much
that he sent his only beloved Son
to save us from sin.
Confident in such love,
let us pray for our needs and the needs of our world:

We pray for an end to violence and hatred;
may forgiving hearts bring healing and peace
to lives shattered by war and unrest.

Silence

Lord, in your mercy:
Change our hearts.

We pray for an end to injustice and poverty;
may forgiving hearts recognise the rights
of every human person created in God's image
to a life of dignity and freedom.

Silence

Lord, in your mercy:
Change our hearts.

We pray for an end to racism and prejudice;
may forgiving hearts build a society
of acceptance and equality,
where no one is judged or condemned
because of the colour of their skin,
their religious beliefs or the way they choose to live.

Silence

Lord, in your mercy:
Change our hearts.

We pray for an end to the careless destruction
of our world and its resources;
may forgiving hearts help us to change our wasteful ways
and to cherish and protect God's gifts of creation,
so that they can be enjoyed and shared by everyone.

Silence

Lord, in your mercy:
Change our hearts.

Knowing that our heavenly Father is listening,
in the silence of our hearts
let us share our own unspoken prayers with him.

Silence

Merciful Father,
forgive our many mistakes,
change our hearts,
and lead us back to your forgiving love.
We ask this in the name of Christ our Lord.
Amen.

32
TIMES OF SADNESS AND REJECTION

Jesus knew how it felt to be sad. He wept at the death of his friend Lazarus; he was plunged into the deepest sorrow in the Garden of Gethsemane; his friends and followers let him down; and those he came to save refused to believe in him. Jesus knew how it felt to be rejected too. He was chased from Nazareth by his own townspeople; condemned to death in favour of the murderer Barabbas; ridiculed for the message of love he came to share with the world; and despised by many of the Pharisees and elders. At times when we feel sad and rejected ourselves, Christ shares those moments of pain in a very special and personal way.

Lord of loneliness and pain

United in love, we gather as brothers and sisters
to pray to our heavenly Father
for our own needs and the needs of the world:

We pray for the Church
and her mission to live and share the Gospel of love;
may we, her people, warmly welcome and encourage
anyone who wishes to walk in the footsteps of Christ.

Silence

Lord of love:
Hear us, we pray.

We pray for people who are shunned by society;
may we imitate the example of Christ
who welcomed tax collectors and sinners,
and gave everyone the chance to fulfil their potential
as children of God.

Silence

Lord of love:
Hear us, we pray.

We pray for those who are persecuted and ridiculed;
may they take courage from the suffering
which Christ endured doing his Father's will,
and be given the strength to make a stand
against injustice and dishonesty in our world.

Silence

Lord of love:
Hear us, we pray.

We pray for those who feel abandoned and alone;
may our heavenly Father comfort and support them

in their hour of need,
as he comforted Jesus in the Garden of Gethsemane.

Silence

Lord of love:
Hear us, we pray.

We pray for all who suffer in mind or body,
and all who are afraid;
may our loving care and friendship
help them to overcome their problems and pain
with dignity and hope.

Silence

Lord of love:
Hear us, we pray.

Knowing that our heavenly Father is listening,
in the silence of our hearts
let us share our own unspoken prayers with him.

Silence

God of love,
you offer friendship to the friendless
and hope to the hopeless.
Touch our hearts
and help us to share the warmth and joy
of your love with the world.
We ask this in the name of Jesus our Lord.
Amen.

Moments of sadness

With love in our hearts,
let us unite as one family to ask God for all our needs:

Christ was driven away
by those who did not listen or understand;
may people who are driven from their homes,
their families and their land
find forgiveness in their hearts
and comfort in their sorrow.

Silence

We pray to the Lord:
Lord, hear us.

Christ was betrayed and let down by his friends;
may we be forgiven
for the times when we betray his friendship
and turn our backs on his love and the love of others.

Silence

We pray to the Lord:
Lord, hear us.

Christ was imprisoned and tortured
for the sake of goodness;
may all who suffer such cruelty and imprisonment
for just causes
be strengthened by their closeness to God
and our cries for their freedom.

Silence

We pray to the Lord:
Lord, hear us.

Christ wept at the death of his friend Lazarus;
may the tears of sadness
of those who mourn for a loved one
become tears of joy
with the promise of their resurrection and eternal life.

Silence

We pray to the Lord:
Lord, hear us.

Christ was laid in the darkness of the tomb;
may those whose lives are overshadowed
by the darkness of despair and tragedy
find fresh hope and comfort
in knowing that nothing is impossible for God.

Silence

We pray to the Lord:
Lord, hear us.

Knowing that our heavenly Father is listening,
in the silence of our hearts
let us share our own unspoken prayers with him.

Silence

Lord God,
we ask you to receive our prayers
and answer them according to your holy will.
We make these prayers through Christ our Lord.
Amen.

33
SUFFERING

Nobody's life is totally free from suffering or pain. It might be something quite unimportant, a little anxiety or worry; or it may be something much greater which can be a heavy burden for us to carry. Jesus said, 'Come to me, all you who labour and are overburdened, and I will give you rest' (Matthew 11:28). These are very comforting words to anyone who is in difficulty or pain. Whether it affects our minds or bodies, none of us enjoy suffering. Jesus told us that to become his followers, we must each take up our own cross in life and carry it. By his own suffering and death, Jesus identifies with our suffering and pain, and made it possible for us to share in his resurrection and eternal life.

Lord of mercy

As children of God,
let us turn to our loving Father
with all our needs and burdens:

Christ touched hearts which were broken;
may his loving presence help us to bring comfort and hope
to all who suffer the cross of sadness or bereavement.

Silence

Lord of mercy:
Hear our prayer.

Christ touched the lives of the lonely and the friendless;
may his loving presence help us to bring friendship and hope
to all who suffer the cross of loneliness.

Silence

Lord of mercy:
Hear our prayer.

Christ touched the eyes of the blind, the ears of the deaf,
and the lips of those who could not speak;
may his loving presence help us to accept and encourage
those who are disabled to live full and active lives;
and help us to become more open-minded
towards those who suffer the cross of misunderstanding.

Silence

Lord of mercy:
Hear our prayer.

Christ touched the pain of the sick;
may his loving presence
help us to strengthen their courage,
and reassure those who suffer the cross of illness.

Silence

Lord of mercy:
Hear our prayer.

Knowing that our heavenly Father is listening,
in the silence of our hearts
let us share our own unspoken prayers with him.

Silence

Merciful Father,
your watchful care and tender love
are unending.
Bring comfort to all who suffer,
and your peace to those
who believe in your love.
Grant this through Christ our Lord.
Amen.

Suffering Saviour

As brothers and sisters in the one family of God,
let us bring our prayers
before our loving Father in heaven:

Jesus suffered the pain of being betrayed and let down;
let those who are betrayed by others
find it in their hearts to forgive them.

Silence

Lord of love:
Heal us.

Jesus suffered the anguish of being rejected and disowned;
let those who are shunned by society
and denied the dignity they deserve
discover our friendship and loving support.

Silence

Lord of love:
Heal us.

Jesus suffered the agony of loneliness and fear;
let those who feel alone and afraid
find the courage and strength to face the future
filled with confidence in their heavenly Father's great love.

Silence

Lord of love:
Heal us.

Jesus suffered the torment of being beaten and abused;
let those who are persecuted and punished
for the sake of justice and truth
find consolation and joy
in knowing that Christ shares their suffering.

Silence

Lord of love:
Heal us.

Jesus suffered and died on the cross;
let those who are dying
find hope and peace
as they prepare to pass from this life
into the kingdom of paradise.

Silence

Lord of love:
Heal us.

Knowing that our heavenly Father is listening,
in the silence of our hearts
let us share our own unspoken prayers with him.

Silence

Almighty God,
may our suffering in life
allow us some share in the suffering and Passion of Jesus,
and bring us closer to his endless love.
We ask this in the name of Christ our Lord.
Amen.

34
TIMES OF FEAR AND ANXIETY

Many different things can make us feel afraid at different times of our lives. We can find ourselves thinking about all sorts of everyday things and events, which can make us feel anxious or worried. What we should remember is that we are God's most precious creation, and he will always take great care of us. He shares every trouble we have, and we are never alone. He makes our burdens and troubles easier to bear and we need never be afraid, because we know, wherever we are and whatever we do, he is always watching over us. God never takes his eyes off us because he loves us so much!

Trust in me

Jesus said,
'Where two or three gather together in my name,
I will be there with them.'
Let us ask God to listen now
as we share our worries and needs with him:

Let us pray for our Christian faith to be strengthened;
that we might have the courage
to proclaim God's saving love everywhere,
knowing that he is watching over us and guiding us.

Silence

Almighty Father:
We trust in you.

Let us pray for those who endure injustice, hunger and poverty;
that they will find hope in God's loving care
through our efforts to relieve their suffering
and answer their cries for help.

Silence

Almighty Father:
We trust in you.

Let us pray for people who are filled with despair and sadness;
that they will find comfort and relief in sharing their burdens,
and by knowing that we love and care for them.

Almighty Father:
We trust in you.

Let us pray for people who have difficult challenges
to overcome in their lives;
that they will cope confidently with any difficulty,
knowing that Christ is watching over them and guiding them.

Almighty Father:
We trust in you.

Let us pray for people who are dying;
that God will strengthen them for their final journey,
so that they are unafraid to make their way
into his heavenly kingdom.

Silence

Almighty Father:
We trust in you.

Let us pray for one another;
that we do not waste time
worrying about unimportant things in life,
but instead concentrate on what matters to God our loving Father.

Silence

Almighty Father:
We trust in you.

Knowing that our heavenly Father is listening,
in the silence of our hearts
let us share our own unspoken prayers with him.

Silence

Father in heaven,
watch over the children
gathered before you in prayer,
and answer us according to your will.
We make our prayers through Christ your Son.
Amen.

35
GOD OF POWER AND MIGHT

We know that God is almighty and all-powerful. He created the world and everything we know within our universe. Throughout the Old Testament there are many stories which tell of the mighty power of God, but it was Jesus, the Son of God made man, who really allowed us to glimpse something of God's true glory and might.

Live in us

Gathered together as one loving family,
we ask our heavenly Father
to listen to the needs of his children:

Jesus made the blind see, the deaf hear, and the voiceless speak;
may he open our eyes to recognise him in those around us,
our ears to hear and understand his Word,
and our voices to proclaim the Good News to the world.

Silence

God of power:
Live in us.

Jesus fed the hungry and quenched those who were thirsty;
may his example inspire us to support aid organisations
which work to ensure that everyone has access
to plentiful food and clean water.

Silence

God of power:
Live in us.

Jesus raised the dead to life;
may Christ, who is the Resurrection and the Life,
raise all who have died to share in his eternal glory.

Silence

God of power:
Live in us.

Jesus cured the sick and took pity on those who suffered;
may we bring comfort and healing
to those who are ill or in pain
by our tender care and friendship.

Silence

God of power:
Live in us.

Knowing that our heavenly Father is listening,
in the silence of our hearts
let us share our own unspoken prayers with him.

Silence

Almighty God,
hear our prayers and change our selfish lives
with your mighty love,
so that we may do your holy will.
Grant this through Christ our Lord.
Amen.

Lord of life

As brothers and sisters in faith,
let us ask God our Father
to listen to our prayers of intercession:

Jesus is the Bread of Life;
may we reveal to the world
the love which Christ shares with us in the Eucharist.

Silence

Lord of life:
Hear our prayer.

Jesus is the Water of Life;
may our thirst for living water
open our minds to God's Word,
our hearts to God's love,
and our lives to do God's will.

Silence

Lord of life:
Hear our prayer.

Jesus is the Resurrection and the Life;
may our brothers and sisters who have died
share the joy and glory of eternal life with him
in the kingdom of heaven.

Silence

Lord of life:
Hear our prayer.

Jesus is the Way and Life;
may we keep his commandments of love
and, filled with his life, follow the way
which leads us to his Father's kingdom.

Silence

Lord of life:
Hear our prayer.

Knowing that our heavenly Father is listening,
in the silence of our hearts
let us share our own unspoken prayers with him.

Silence

Living God,
as we draw life from you,
unite us in love,
and strengthen us to share
your life with the world.
We make our prayer through Christ
who is Lord for ever and ever.
Amen.

Jesus brings new life

Jesus taught us to call God 'Our Father'
and to ask him for all our needs.
So, with confidence in this great love,
we pray for ourselves and others:

That the leaders of all nations
will uphold and respect the dignity of life,
and strive to improve its quality for all people.

Silence

Merciful Father:
Renew our lives.

That lives which are broken and damaged
by violence and war
will be given the chance to be rebuilt and healed
in an atmosphere of peace and reconciliation.

Silence

Merciful Father:
Renew our lives.

That those who struggle with guilt and sin
will allow God's loving forgiveness to change their hearts,
so that they may begin life afresh in his love.

Silence

Merciful Father:
Renew our lives.

That the promise of eternal life
will fill us with joy and confidence
as we follow the footsteps of Christ our Saviour
throughout our lives.

Silence

Merciful Father:
Renew our lives.

Knowing that our heavenly Father is listening,
in the silence of our hearts
let us share our own unspoken prayers with him.

Silence

Living Lord,
may your life bubble up inside us like a spring,
flooding our lives with love and forgiveness,
and bringing us ever closer to you.
We ask this through Christ our Lord.
Amen.

36
FOOD AND DRINK

The Gospel stories often tell of Jesus eating and drinking with people. In those days, as today, to share a meal with someone was a declaration of friendship and trust, and an expression of our love for one another. Jesus often angered the Pharisees by dining with 'sinners' and outcasts, but he did this as a clear sign of his acceptance and love for others. Food and drink are essential for life, and without them our bodies quickly become sick and weak. Jesus described himself as the 'Bread of Life' (John 6:35), and shared his life with the world by feeding us with his own Body and Blood. Through the Eucharist, we receive the living Bread from heaven and the gift of his eternal life.

Hunger for God

Jesus told us that we are very precious to God,
and he will always take care of all our needs.
So we turn to him now with our concerns as we pray:

For people who hunger not for food
but for peace that comes from a pure and forgiving heart.

Silence

Loving Father:
Hear our prayer.

For people who thirst not for water
but for justice and respect for the dignity of the poor.

Silence

Loving Father:
Hear our prayer.

For people who hunger not for wealth
but the richness of being loved and accepted for what they are.

Silence

Loving Father:
Hear our prayer.

For people who thirst not for water
but to hear the Word of God and to know the person of Jesus.

Silence

Loving Father:
Hear our prayer.

For people who hunger not for food
but the faith to believe that God loves them,
and they can trust completely in his care.

Silence

Loving Father:
Hear our prayer.

Knowing that our heavenly Father is listening,
in the silence of our hearts
let us share our own unspoken prayers with him.

Silence

Heavenly Father,
listen to the prayers of the family gathered before you.
May we trust in your infinite love,
and try not to worry unnecessarily
about whatever the future might hold.
We ask you to grant our prayers
through Christ your Son.
Amen.

Lord, feed us

Gathered together in love,
as brothers and sisters in Christ,
let us ask our loving Father in heaven
to listen to our needs:

We pray for the Church throughout the world;
that Christ will feed us with God's Word,
and make us grow in wisdom and faith.

Silence

Lord God:
Feed your people.

We pray for people who hunger for freedom,
justice and equality;
that Christ will feed them with his own life,
and give us the courage and strength
to defend and protect the rights of all God's children.

Silence

Lord God:
Feed your people.

We pray for people who hunger and thirst
for an end to war and hatred;
that Christ will feed them with his Body and Blood,
poured out to bring peace and forgiveness for all.

Silence

Lord God:
Feed your people.

We pray for those who have died;
that Christ the Living Bread will raise them
to new life and eternal happiness
in God's heavenly kingdom.

Silence

Lord God:
Feed your people.

We pray for ourselves and the familes gathered here today;
that we may always be ready
to share whatever we have with others,
accepting nothing in return
except the joy which comes from serving one another.

Silence

Lord God:
Feed your people.

Knowing that our heavenly Father is listening,
in the silence of our hearts
let us share our own unspoken prayers with him.

Silence

Father in heaven,
you shower us with gifts and lovingly watch over us.
May this Eucharist fill us with life and love,
so that you may live in us
and we may live in you.
Grant this through Christ our Lord.
Amen.

The Bread of Life

With love in our hearts for God and one another,
let us pray together:

For the Church and all our faithful brothers and sisters;
that Jesus the Bread of Life
will unite all Christian people in love and thanksgiving.

Silence

Lord of life:
Live in us.

For peace in our homes and our world;
that Jesus the Bread of Life
will grant all people the peace and joy of God's kingdom.

Silence

Lord of life:
Live in us.

For those who have died and rest in peace;
that Jesus the Bread of Life
will raise all who have shared this one bread and one cup
to the glory of eternal life.

Silence

Lord of life:
Live in us.

For people who are in any kind of need or trouble;
that Jesus the Bread of Life will inspire us
to share all that we have and are
with those who need our love and help.

Silence

Lord of life:
Live in us.

For the family gathered here today
to celebrate this Eucharist;
that Jesus the Bread of Life,
who offered himself to his Father,
will help us to offer our lives to serve God and one another.

Silence

Lord of life:
Live in us.

Knowing that our heavenly Father is listening,
in the silence of our hearts
let us share our own unspoken prayers with him.

Silence

Almighty God,
through the bread and cup we offer,
may we be filled with life
and united in our love
for you and for one another.
We make our prayers through Christ our Lord.
Amen.

37
HARVEST

God provides everything that is necessary for his creation to be fruitful and multiply. Just as the crops of the field produce a rich harvest, so too can the Word of God planted in our hearts yield a rich harvest as we bear the fruits of his love in our daily thoughts and actions.

God of the harvest

God our heavenly Father loves us
and provides for all our needs.
With faith in his tender care,
let us join in praying together
for the concerns and troubles we share:

Let us pray for the Church and all who follow Christ;
may we bear the fruit of God's Word and love
in our daily lives
by seeing with the eyes of Christ,
by speaking with the words of Christ,
and by loving with the heart of Christ.

Silence

Heavenly Father:
May we bear the fruits of your love.

Let us pray for people
whose lives are choked with greed and selfishness;
may God's love change their hearts
and help them to bear the fruits of generosity,
kindness and compassion.

Silence

Heavenly Father:
May we bear the fruits of your love.

Let us pray for people
whose lives are diseased by hatred and anger;
may God's loving peace heal their wounds and pain,
and help them to bear the fruits of forgiveness and understanding.

Silence

Heavenly Father:
May we bear the fruits of your love.

Let us pray for people
who are touched by any kind of suffering or sadness;
may their pain help the fruits of their faith
to grow strong and vigorous,
like the vine which is pruned by the master gardener.

Silence

Heavenly Father:
May we bear the fruits of your love.

Let us pray for those who have died in faith;
may their death, like the grain of wheat,
give rise to new life in God's heavenly kingdom.

Silence

Heavenly Father:
May we bear the fruits of your love.

Knowing that our heavenly Father is listening,
in the silence of our hearts
let us share our own unspoken prayers with him.

Silence

God our Father, Creator of all life,
we thank you for all your generous gifts.
May our lives always be pleasing to you
and produce a rich harvest in your kingdom of love.
We ask this through Christ our Lord.
Amen.

38
GIFTS FROM GOD

When we love someone, one way of expressing that love is by giving him or her gifts to use and enjoy. God has given us many gifts as a sign of his great love for his children: the gift of creation and all its wonders; the unique talents we each have; the Holy Spirit and the special gifts he offers; and the greatest gift of all, his Son Jesus Christ, the Bread of Life and Saviour of the world.

The gifts of the Spirit

Jesus said, 'When two or three gather in my name,
I will be there with them.'
Let us ask him to bring our needs and worries
before God our Father:

Let us ask for the gift of understanding
in the Christian Church;
may we work together in harmony
to bear the fruits of God's love in our world.

Silence

Lord, hear us:
Send your Spirit.

Let us ask for the gift of wisdom
for governments and people in authority;
may they strive to bear the fruits of peace
for their own nations and the nations of our world.

Silence

Lord, hear us:
Send your Spirit.

Let us ask for the gift of courage;
may we, God's people, be brave enough
to bear the fruits of faithfulness,
as we witness to his Gospel of love.

Silence

Lord, hear us:
Send your Spirit.

Let us ask for the gift of awe and wonder;
may our sense of amazement
at our wonderful world and all its creatures

bear the fruits of joy
as we delight in what we have been given.

Silence

Lord, hear us:
Send your Spirit.

Knowing that our heavenly Father is listening,
in the silence of our hearts
let us share our own unspoken prayers with him.

Silence

Loving Father,
fill us with the power of your Holy Spirit,
so that the gifts you so generously give
may help your kingdom to grow.
Grant this in the name of Christ our Lord and Saviour.
Amen.

Gifts to use

As we gather before God our Father,
we ask him to hear and answer the needs of all his people:

Let us pray for peace in our troubled world;
may we use the gift of our talents
to promote peace in our homes, our schools
and our everyday lives.

Silence

Loving Lord:
Let us do your will.

Let us pray for the homeless and hungry;
may we use the gift of our talents wisely
to relieve suffering and hardship.

Silence

Loving Lord:
Let us do your will.

Let us pray for people who are disabled in mind or body;
may we use the gift of our talents
to help them overcome their difficulties
and give them every opportunity
to live and enjoy life to the full.

Silence

Loving Lord:
Let us do your will.

Let us pray for people who feel hopeless and alone;
may we use the gift of our talents
to help them to feel valued,
and to realise that every individual
has something good to offer to the world.

Silence

Loving Lord:
Let us do your will.

Knowing that our heavenly Father is listening,
in the silence of our hearts
let us share our own unspoken prayers with him.

Silence

God of goodness,
may we use the gifts you have given wisely,
so that they may bring us closer
to your loving kingdom.
We ask this through Christ our Lord.
Amen.

Gifts of creation

As we remember God's love for us,
let us pray in the Spirit of Christ
for the needs of the world:

We pray that we will cherish and respect God's world,
taking care to use its resources wisely,
avoiding pollution and unnecessary waste.

Silence

Lord, in your mercy:
Hear our prayer.

We pray that the destruction of war
will belong to the past,
through our efforts to encourage peace and forgiveness.

Silence

Lord, in your mercy:
Hear our prayer.

We pray that hunger will be satisfied and poverty destroyed,
as countries which have plenty
share their resources and technology
with those which have little.

Silence

Lord, in your mercy:
Hear our prayer.

We pray that we will always respect and protect God's gift of life,
remembering to treat one another with the dignity
which every person created in his likeness deserves.

Silence

Lord, in your mercy:
Hear our prayer.

Knowing that our heavenly Father is listening,
in the silence of our hearts
let us share our own unspoken prayers with him.

Silence

All-powerful God,
creator of the universe and creator of humanity,
your gifts of love bring us life and joy.
Help us always to treasure and appreciate
what we have so generously been given.
We make our prayers through Jesus Christ your Son.
Amen.

INDEX

References are to theme rather than page numbers

ORDINARY TIME

YEAR B

ADVENT

YEAR C

ADVENT

CHRISTMAS

LENT

EASTER

ORDINARY TIME

SPECIAL FEASTS – YEARS A, B, C

8202

P217